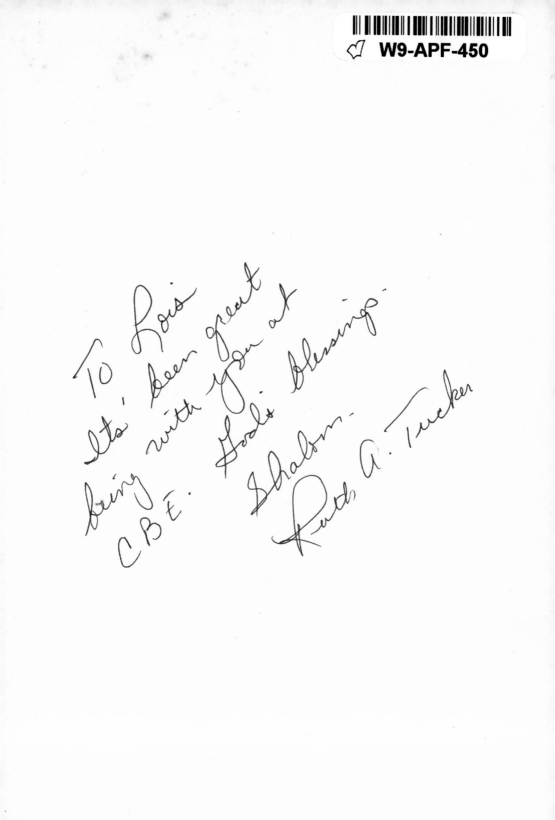

TO Lois
Its' been great
being with you at
CBE. God's blessings.
Shalom.
Ruth A. Tucker

MULTIPLE CHOICES

Other Books by Ruth A. Tucker

From Jerusalem to Irian Jaya: A Biographical History of Christian Missions

Daughters of the Church: Women and Ministry from New Testament Times to the Present (with Walter L. Liefeld)

Guardians of the Great Commission: The Story of Women in Modern Missions

Another Gospel: Alternative Religions and the New Age Movement

Private Lives of Pastors' Wives

Christian Speakers' Treasury: A Sourcebook of Anecdotes and Quotes

Stories of Faith: 365 Daily Devotions, Inspirational Episodes from the Lives of Christians

Women in the Maze: Questions and Answers on Biblical Equality

A Guide for Women

MULTIPLE CHOICES

Making Wise Decisions in a Complicated World

Ruth A. Tucker

ZondervanPublishingHouse

Grand Rapids, Michigan

A Division of HarperCollinsPublishers

Multiple Choices
Copyright © 1992 by Ruth A. Tucker

Requests for information should be addressed to:
Zondervan Publishing House
Grand Rapids, Michigan 49530

International Trade Paper Edition ISBN 0-310-60451-6

Library of Congress Cataloging-in-Publication Data

Tucker, Ruth A., 1945–
   Multiple choices / Ruth A. Tucker.
     p. cm.
   ISBN 0-310-54920-5 (hardcover)
   1. Women—Conduct of life. 2. Women—Religious life. 3. Choice
(Psychology) 4. Women in the Bible. I. Title.
BJ1610.T83   1992
248.8'43—dc20   92–15328
                                                   CIP

Edited by Judith Markham
Cover designed by Terry Dugan

Printed in the United States of America

92 93 94 95 96 97 / BP / 10 9 8 7 6 5 4 3 2 1

To
Joyce Doll Hagen,
my "blood sister" and confidant
since second grade.
With love and gratitude
for forty years of friendship

Contents

Introduction

Predestination versus free will. This was a debate I grew up on and one I still have not entirely settled in my own mind—except to recognize that both sides offer profound truth. God is sovereign and rules the universe, but at the same time we are free to make our own choices. Even in our decision to serve God we are free to choose, as Joshua reminded the Israelites: "Choose you this day whom ye will serve . . . but as for me and my house, we will serve the LORD" (Josh. 24:15 KJV).

Freedom to choose is a right most Americans take for granted. Few of us can even imagine what it would be like to live in a country with no real freedom. Yet we fear the loss of freedom and go to war to protect it.

But in some respects freedom to choose has become a curse. It was freedom of choice that allowed Adam and Eve to sin in the first place, and their choice set the course for all sin from that day forward.

Even on a mundane level freedom of choice can be more of a burden than a blessing. Some time ago I heard a news story of a Russian woman visiting relatives in the United States. They took her to a mall, thinking she would be in shoppers' heaven. Instead, the outing became a traumatic ordeal for the visitor, complicated by a throbbing headache and shortness of breath. The problem? Too many choices. Imagine having twenty styles and colors of shoes to choose from when all your life even one style and color—that fit— has been a luxury.

Freedom to choose truly is a prized asset, but it also has its down side. "Free at last, free at last" rings the heart-stirring refrain from the lips of Martin Luther King. Indeed we are free—men and women, black and white. We have freedom of religion and freedom of speech and freedom of the press. But we also have freedom to smoke and freedom to abort a baby and freedom to divorce and freedom to make a host of other unwise decisions.

"Man is condemned to be free," wrote Jean-Paul Sartre, the great French existentialist. "Condemned because he did not create himself, yet is nevertheless at liberty, and from the moment that he is thrown into this world he is responsible for everything he does."[1]

Sartre's picture of life is pessimistic, to say the least, and is surely not a Christian worldview. We are on our own; according to his scenario, God is not an active participant. Yet it is a picture that contains more than an element of truth. Sartre goes on to say, "Man is nothing else but what he purposes"—what he chooses—"nothing else but the sum of his actions."[2]

In a very real sense we are the sum total of our choices. For Christians this has special meaning. As we *search* to *find* the will of God for our lives, we would do well to realize that God's will is not a veiled revelation to be discovered (as we are often told in seminars and books on "finding" the will of God). No, the will of God unfolds naturally as we make right choices. Still, that is an awesome truth considering the fact that every hour of the day we are faced with multiple choices.

For women the relentless reality of multiple choices can sometimes be overwhelming. We are living in a complicated world that pulls us in every direction. For single women marriage or career advancement can often seem a conflicting choice. For married women it's frequently a decision of when to have children, with a watchful eye on the biological clock. And for mothers the conflict may be whether or not to work outside the home—or to devise a compromise solution. The choices are endless and often frustrating.

Until quite recently, women lived with many restrictions when it came to decision making, their freedom to choose severely limited by sexual and cultural boundaries. In fact, in many parts of the world this is still the case. But for North American women, life in the 1990s offers almost limitless options. Today, as never before, we are confronted with an incredible array of choices that offer an endless variety in lifestyle and vocation.

In the past, higher education was considered a "male" province and thus denied to women, as were many professions as well as political and economic independence. Not so today. Diversity and opportunity abound for females of all ages. Little girls quickly realize that playing first base is just as appropriate as playing dress-up with Mommy's high heels and makeup. Fashion reflects these lifestyle options. From blue jeans and sweats to tailored suits and ruffles, woman have wide-ranging choices.

Career counseling classes in high school quickly demonstrate this diversification. A girl can freely express her preference for virtually any vocation; indeed, she's proud to say that she is planning to enter the field of sports medicine or engineering or corporate law. Adult lifestyles also offer women many more options. This is especially true of married women with children, who can choose to be full-time homemakers, to work part-time, or to work full-time.

We only have to read accounts of slave women or pioneer women or factory women to be reminded of the lack of options available to our ancestors. Today, however, even allowing for government cutbacks, social programs and educational opportunities provide options for economically disadvantaged women if they are willing to take the initiative, make a decision, and seek out the help that is available.

What a tragedy when we become convinced that we are so trapped in our circumstances that life holds no real positive choices for us. Who ought to exhibit that mentality more than a black mother in a crime and drug infested ghetto? Don't preach choice to her, some will say. But Rantine McKesson from Detroit, pictured on the cover of *Time* magazine, proves otherwise. "THE SUCCESS OF OUR COMMUNITY DEPENDS ON ME" proclaim the words on her T-shirt. When law enforcement and government programs did not come to her aid, she made the choice to act on her own. She organized a march and challenged neighbors to get involved, and they did. In similar fashion Los Angeles women have banded together to form MAGIC—Mothers Against Gangs in Communities. They are women who have looked at their options and chosen to be survivors, not victims.[3]

Whatever a woman's social standing, she does well to seek variety and options in her life, so that whether times are good or times are tough, her choices will serve her well. And in those choices we must be women of vision.

A woman of vision sees opportunities where others see discouragement. She is able to put her own situation in perspective. She sees others who are worse off than she and reaches out to help. She does not minimize her own problems, but neither does she exaggerate them. Most of all, she maintains a mental storehouse of options ready to draw on when they are needed.

Who is this woman? The Bible provides a model in Proverbs 31.

The Proverbs 31 woman was capable and well organized; but beyond that she had the freedom to make choices. She was valued by her husband and was a person in her own right, strong and self-confident. Despite the many restrictions her culture placed on her, she drew strength from the opportunities available and reveled in her accomplishments.

Indeed, she seems to be a woman completely comfortable with her sexuality. She was neither threatened by, nor a threat to, her husband, who had "full confidence in her" (v. 11) and praised her (v. 28). She was self-assured— "clothed with strength and dignity"—and was a good-natured optimist who could "laugh at the days to come" (v. 25). She was a wise woman and did not keep that wisdom to herself; in addition to all her other duties, she was a teacher—"faithful instruction is on her tongue" (v. 26). On a day-to-day basis she considered the options open to her and made wise choices accordingly.

Was this "superwoman" for real, or is she simply an ideal, far beyond the grasp of the average woman? It is significant that we are not told this woman's name, which seems to indicate that she may represent women collectively rather than one specific woman. Real or ideal, however, she does offer a model or prototype for today's women. Because women today feel torn in many directions by the multifaceted world in which we live, the Proverbs 31 woman is a figure with whom many of us can identify.

The purpose of this book is to encourage women to rise to the challenge of life's tough choices. Each chapter opens with a multiple-choice question relating to a woman of the Bible. The choices given do not necessarily include *the* right answer, and there is no key in the back of the book with all the right answers. Rather they illustrate the mixed emotions and mixed motives we often have to deal with in the difficult process of decision making.

This is a book about making choices. About making wise decisions in a complex, complicated, and often frightening world.

But how can I possibly write a book on making wise decisions? When I reflect back over my own life, I must readily concede that many decisions I have made have not been right ones. In some cases I was naive; in others self-centered or overly confident or even shortsighted. Yet I have learned from those wrong choices, and many of them—through God's grace—have been redeemed. Some wrongs can never be made right, of course: sinful choices, hurtful choices. But wrong choices can be retrieved and redirected if we apply the right principles.

Above all, we must recognize that our lives are not simply the sum of our choices, as Sartre would suggest. We are finite beings whose lives are fashioned by a loving and infinite Creator. Our joys and sorrows are often entirely unrelated to our own choices. Our free will is balanced by God's sovereignty. Our choices—minor and momentous— are woven together with "Amazing Grace" into a living tapestry designed by an almighty God.

My life is but a weaving, between my God and me,
I do not choose the colors, He worketh steadily,
Oftimes He weaveth sorrow, and I in foolish pride,
Forget He sees the upper, and I the underside.
Not till the loom is silent, and shuttles cease to fly,
Will God unroll the canvas and explain the reason why.
The dark threads are as needful in the skillful Weaver's hand
As the threads of gold and silver in the pattern He has planned.
—Anonymous

One

Impossible Choices

God's will for our lives unfolds through choices that: **(a)** *never force us into ethical or moral gray areas,* **(b)** *have an obvious right solution,* **(c)** *always have clear answers in Scripture,* **(d)** *all of the above,* **(e)** *none of the above.*

As *I sit at my computer* at this very moment, I am conscious of the necessity of applying right principles in decision making. And I am reminded once again of how difficult and agonizing life's choices can be. I have just returned from a short Labor Day vacation at my childhood home in Northern Wisconsin. It was to be a relaxing time of visiting family and friends, canoeing, hiking through the woods I roamed in my youth, and even sneaking away by myself with a paper and pencil to mull over some of the issues I had been struggling with in writing this book. Instead, my vacation turned into a laboratory for "multiple choices."

One of my first stops was the home of my "blood sister" Joyce. We had been best friends from second grade through high school, and it had been more than a year since we had seen each other. But my unannounced appearance had a stunning effect. Only hours earlier Joyce had concluded that she needed to talk to me, and there I stood! Joyce had helped me through a difficult time in my own life a few years earlier, and now she needed me. I was someone she could confide in—someone who could identify with the enormity of the problem and offer advice and compassion.

The crisis involved Joyce's daughter Tina. This should

15

have been a high point in Tina's life. She was the mother of a three-week-old boy, Caleb, her first child, planned for and eagerly anticipated. Instead, her life was unraveling. She felt like an animal trapped in a cage with no way of escape.

Two years earlier Tina had found her tall, dark, and handsome Prince Charming, the son of a minister. Their six-month courtship had not been entirely without friction, but her fiancé was quick to smooth over their differences with flowers.

During the course of their two-year marriage, however, the flowers of promise had wilted. In their place were planted seeds of suspicion that rapidly germinated into ugly weeds which invaded the garden of their marriage.

Could it really be true that the man Tina thought she would share the rest of her life with was not the person he had claimed to be? He was a professing Christian. How could he have so deliberately deceived her? And how could she have been so naive? The questions flooded her mind. Had he really been dispatched only weeks earlier on a one-day mission to Saudi Arabia to lead a tiny band of Navy Seals into Iraq to kill Saddam Hussein's top advisors? It seemed impossible. But if he was not there, as he claimed, where was he during that mysterious absence?

And what about his past military career? Had he really distinguished himself in secret military missions all over the world? Had he actually received a Purple Heart and a Congressional Medal of Honor? Or were these stories all fabrications too? One question led to another. What about all the supplies and equipment he had brought home from work that, he said, had been "given" to him by his boss? And what about the $500 check for a carpentry job that had been made out to him personally instead of to his employer? Tina clung to the desperate hope that there might be explanations for all this, but in her heart she knew better.

To complicate matters, Tina was afraid of her husband.

He had never physically abused her, but he frequently made offhanded threats about killing people; he abused animals, and his military fantasies involved strangling and slitting people's throats.

What should she do? What was the *right* choice in a situation like this? *Was* there a right choice? As a Christian seeking to do the will of God she was distraught. Before her was what seemed to be a series of impossible choices.

As I became involved in the decision making with Joyce and Tina, it became apparent that Tina was dealing with a multiple-choice problem, like one of those mind-boggling questions we have all confronted on a final exam. In fact, there seemed to be no *right* answer. Yet even without a right answer, Tina had begun applying some right principles in dealing with this awful predicament.

Her first step had been to confront her husband about the apparent thefts from his place of employment. When her questions elicited only denials, she confided in those closest to her—her parents—and together with them sought help from close friends and her minister.

Disclosing suspicions of wrongdoing might seem like an obvious step, but many wives in this situation would be tempted to remain silent and cover up the problems, hoping to avoid personal and public humiliation. Women often fool themselves into believing the problems will go away. Also, they sometimes feel bound by such an unreasonable sense of loyalty that they refuse to "betray" their marriage partner; or they distort the meaning of submission and thereby become accomplices to wrongdoing, and in the process facilitate dysfunctional or sinful behavior.

For Tina, disclosure was the only course. For two years, despite troubling suspicions, she had continued to believe in her husband. But now the evidence was mounting, and she had to act. She had to investigate matters herself so that she would be better equipped to make informed and intelligent choices.

With her parents' help, Tina contacted military personnel and learned that her husband had not been in a special military force nor had he won medals of honor. From his former employer she learned that the items he claimed were given to him had actually been stolen. And from his former fiancée, whom she had never talked to before, she learned that he had a long history of deceit, dishonesty, and bizarre behavior.

Believing there was still hope that her husband might break down, acknowledge the truth, and recognize his need for professional psychiatric care, Tina's parents and pastor made one last effort to confront him with the facts. His response was to jump into his truck and head for home to get Tina. When her parents warned her by phone, Tina fled with the baby to a friend's house and began taking steps to protect herself and her child. She obtained an attorney and contacted the Department of Social Services about possible financial assistance.

As difficult as this initial period of crisis was, in the process Tina found herself gaining strength as she took charge of the situation. She was no longer a victim living alone in her own secret world of fear and suspicions. She had reached out for help and to help herself and was fortified by the support, love, and prayers of her family and close friends.

Prayer was vital in this process. Tina believed in prayer, and she pleaded with God for guidance, though she never assumed that because she had prayed about a particular course of action she automatically had God's blessing. Indeed, every step was taken with reluctance and uncertainty.

Initially Tina decided to file for divorce. Considering her own views on divorce and the inevitable response from the people in the fundamentalist Baptist church she attended, this was a difficult decision. How could she justify such an action? Hadn't she vowed to stand by her husband "for better or for worse"? Yes, she had, and that weighed heavily on her conscience. On the other hand, hadn't he grossly misrepresented himself? He was not the individual he had claimed to be.

But there was far more involved than misrepresentation. Even after the proof was set before him, her husband continued to deny wrongdoing; and his long history, coupled with his refusal to accept any type of counseling, suggested little likelihood of a lasting turnaround. Above all, Tina feared for her life and the life of her child. Nightmares and fantasies of violence were so much a part of her husband's psyche that it would be a risk to continue living with him. To file for separation, she reasoned, would only prolong the ordeal and might encourage him to harass her even more.

I advised Tina to consider annulment. In Michigan, where I live, an annulment can be obtained on the basis of false representation. But Tina's attorney quickly informed her that annulment was not an option in Wisconsin.

Divorce seemed her only recourse, and her parents supported her in that decision. But when word of Tina's intentions reached the leaders of her church, they voiced strong opposition. The Bible, they argued, did not permit divorce in her situation; a separation, perhaps, but not a divorce. If she were to pursue that course she would be disciplined, though what precisely that would entail she was not told. She was, however, asked not to play the piano for the Sunday service, as she normally did, because the pastor had been warned by a couple in the church that they would not come if she did. Interestingly, nothing was said about her husband being disciplined for his actions.

How should Tina respond to the pastor and the church

board? They were all men. Could they really identify with the fear and turmoil she was going through? Were they infallible in their interpretation of Scripture? There were other Christian churches that would not be so judgmental nor take such a dogmatic stance on the issue of divorce. She could find a community of faith elsewhere.

But Tina decided to abide by the verdict of the church leaders. She would file for a separation rather than a divorce. Here again she applied a principle that ought to be a high priority in making right choices: submit to the authority of church leaders.

For many in this era of independence and liberation such a decision seems a sign of weakness—a foolish choice—but I don't think so. Tina had become a part of that local church body by choice, heartily agreeing with its uncompromising stance on doctrinal and social issues. For her to leave and go to another church simply to suit her own purposes would not only be a repudiation of legitimate spiritual authority, but would also separate her from those who truly cared about her. If at a later date she came to the realization that this church was not meeting her needs, then a change might be in order. Or if she later decided that a separation was not right, that could also be changed.

Another major issue Tina faced in the days following her separation was her financial situation. She had a tiny baby to care for, and her estranged husband was now out of work and facing criminal charges. She visited the Department of Social Services, but seeking welfare assistance was repugnant to her.

Again I offered advice—or rather, an opinion. I pay taxes, as do Tina's parents and Tina herself in the past. None of us wanted our tax money to go exclusively for bombs or politicians or even highway repair. We pay taxes, in part, as a safety net for those in society who are in need, and Tina certainly met that qualification.

Tina was determined that public assistance would not become a way of life for her, so even as she was applying for help, she was enquiring about the possibility of further schooling. This meant she was applying another principle of wise decision making: focus on long-range goals. Too often people in crisis become so entangled in the daily swirl of events that they fail to contemplate the future. Tina, however, immediately began planning for the future. Above all, she wanted to finish her college education. Now might be the time to complete what she had left undone, and at the same time begin the healing of her wounded self-image.

But a healthy self-image does not come merely from a college degree or other forms of self-improvement. We are made in the image of God, and the healthiest self-image is one that reflects that image. God's very essence radiates outward, and so must ours. Unfortunately an outward focus is usually the least of our concerns when we are over-whelmed with our own problems. We become utterly self-centered—seemingly with good reason. Yet reaching out to other hurting people can put our own pain in perspective and offer that true sense of self-worth when it is most needed. In keeping with this, I challenged Tina to make time in her busy schedule to reach out to others—perhaps to a lonely person in the nearby nursing home or to a neighbor who needed encouragement.

None of this guarantees happiness, of course. Happiness, to a large degree, is a choice. Indeed, it is a momentous choice. Our happiness affects our physical, spiritual, and mental health and touches every area of our lives. For Tina, happiness did not seem an option. She was distraught, as would be expected. But I knew it was essential that she make a concerted effort to look at the bright side of life and even to laugh, if possible, at the utter absurdity of the circumstances. And so we sometimes found ourselves laughing until we cried as we sat around the table during that Labor Day weekend.

Guilt was another factor restraining Tina's sense of well-being. Why hadn't she delayed the marriage, as her folks had counseled? Why hadn't she recognized the magnitude of the problems earlier? She loved little Caleb, but in light of her growing suspicions would it have been better to have waited longer before getting pregnant? Even her parents struggled with guilt. Joyce was tormented by the fact that she had been "stupid" enough to believe her son-in-law's tales of military exploits, especially his one-day mission to Saudi Arabia and Iraq.

Guilt serves a legitimate purpose in our lives, but in this case I sensed Tina and her folks were berating themselves too much. Tina's husband had become part of the family, and their feelings of trust, loyalty, and love had repressed any tendency toward skepticism and doubt. And that is not all bad. Had Tina's parents been critical and suspicious, they might have later wondered if they had aggravated the problem. As it is, they have the satisfaction of knowing they were not guilty of pointing an accusing finger and meddling in their daughter's marriage.

Tina and her folks also needed assurance that they were not alone in their bizarre crisis. Since we knew of no available support group, I suggested M. Scott Peck's book, *People of the Lie*, in which Peck, a practicing psychiatrist and professing Christian, focuses on a category of mentally ill people whom he describes as "evil": people who are "coherent and self-possessed, holding down responsible jobs, making money, apparently functioning smoothly in the social system, and hardly identifiable on superficial inspection as the least bit deranged." They usually do not suffer themselves, but inflict great pain on others. They "direct at least as much energy into their devious rationalizations and destructive compensations as the healthiest do in loving behavior. Why? What possesses them, drives them? Basically, it is fear. They are terrified that the pretense will break down and they will be exposed to the world and to themselves. They are continually frightened that they will come face-to-face with their own evil."[1]

Peck's book not only gave Tina greater insight into her husband's psychological makeup, but also reassured her that she was not to blame for his pathological behavior, nor could she have prevented it. The book also helped her understand why she had not been able to recognize his mental disorder during their courtship. But no book could erase entirely the sense of failure she felt in having made a wrong choice in her marriage. Had she used the same principles then that she was using now, would the outcome have been entirely different?

Tina's story illustrates the difficulty of making choices when all the options seem bad—like the multiple-choice question that has no right answers. But some of life's multiple-choice questions are the opposite. Sometimes all the answers appear to be right. When, for example, the options include a grant for further schooling, a job promotion, or time out to start a family, how do we make the right choice? Often the same principles apply as when the options are all negative, but the stress of decision making remains.

What are these principles?

First we must acknowledge that life is complex. As Christians we are often tempted to simplify the issues and see everything in black and white. After all, the Bible is our guide, and if we just follow the Bible we can't go wrong. But the Bible itself is a complex volume. It was written at different times and in different places for different people, and sometimes what seems to be approved in one situation is disapproved in a similar situation. Added to that is the guidance of the Holy Spirit. Great men and women of

God—seemingly guided by the Holy Spirit—have differed significantly on the same issues.

Second we must actively seek the mind of God for our own particular situation. This is the most difficult aspect of decision making. It is all too easy to personalize our circumstances to the point of rationalizing that what is wrong for others is right for us. But by the same token we can go to the other extreme if we do not recognize that we are all unique persons with unique circumstances. And God sees us that way. We are not simply sets of social security numbers on income tax tables that fall into specific categories with identical payments due.

Finally we must realize that we will inevitably make wrong choices, but that wrong choices can be made right or at least redirected. We need to continually evaluate the choices we are making and be prepared to admit we have gotten off course, if that is the case. Few choices are entirely irreversible.

Life is filled with multiple choices—sometimes "impossible" choices. We cannot escape them. We can only prepare ourselves for the challenge. As we examine the choices made by women in the Bible, we are able to discern principles that we can apply to our situations today. We are not alone, and the decisions we face are not new. And it is important to realize that we are never expected to make that once-for-all, one-time-only-decision that determines the will of God for our lives. What we are to do is to make a succession of choices that will fashion us into true women of God as his will unfolds.

The ultimate goal in making right choices is not to *find* the will of God, but to *do* the will of God; to have a sense that our lives have purpose, and that in the end the Lord will say, "Well done, good and faithful servant!" We want to have the assurance that our cumulative efforts in life— efforts that may have worn us to a frazzle—will amount to more than wood, hay, and straw, which in the end simply get burned up. Paul's warning about this in 1 Corinthians 3:12 is powerful, and it troubles me sometimes. I must be continually asking myself if all my productivity is of lasting quality, like gold, silver, and precious stones; or if it will end up being burned on the scrap heap of eternity.

This warning is not to be mistaken for a threat of hell. Paul makes it clear that the purpose of this particular fire is to "test the quality" of each person's work (1 Cor. 3:13). In the end, while believers or "builders," to use the apostle's metaphor, may lose their work, they will not lose their souls, but will be saved "as one escaping through the flames." But imagine standing before God someday and having all your life's "accomplishments" burned up!

The Christian life is one choice laid on top of another, like building blocks; choices that determine what kind of structure we will end up with on Judgment Day. Each single choice may not seem of much consequence, but one building block out of place can potentially bring the whole structure crashing down.

Sometimes our choices are momentous ones—not adequately described in the building-block category—that radically change the entire course of our lives. These are ones we make when we are standing at the fork of a road. The decision to marry or stay single, or the decision to be a stockbroker or a missionary (the choice now confronting my seventeen-year-old son) are examples of choices that fall into this category. In such cases it is often tempting to follow the path of least resistance—to follow the crowd or go with the flow.

When we reach one of these turning points, we must force ourselves to pause and reflect on life and seek the mind of God. We must weigh the options and be careful to shun those subtle, subconscious voices telling us *all my friends are getting married, and if I don't marry my life will be miserable* or *if I make a lot of money and accumulate a lot of things, I will be happy.* In these circumstances we desperately need the wisdom of God to guide us, because our choices will make all the difference, as Robert Frost so powerfully portrayed in his poem "The Road Not Taken." May we be women of right-road choices as we make our way through the "yellow wood" of life.

> *Two roads diverged in a yellow wood,*
> *And sorry I could not travel both*
> *And be one traveler, long I stood*
> *And looked down one as far as I could*
> *To where it bent in the undergrowth;*
>
> *Then took the other, as just as fair,*
> *And having perhaps the better claim,*
> *Because it was grassy and wanted wear;*
> *Though as for that the passing there*
> *Had worn them really about the same,*
>
> *And both that morning equally lay*
> *In leaves no step had trodden black,*
> *Oh, I kept the first for another day!*
> *Yet knowing how way leads on to way,*
> *I doubted if I should ever come back.*
>
> *I shall be telling this with a sigh*
> *Somewhere ages and ages hence;*
> *Two roads diverged in a wood, and I—*
> *I took the one less traveled by,*
> *And that has made all the difference.*

—*Robert Frost*
"The Road Not Taken"

Two

Enduring Choices

When Eve was tempted with the forbidden fruit, she should have: **(a)** *told Satan to talk to the man of the house,* **(b)** *consulted Adam privately before making a decision,* **(c)** *told Adam to "just say no,"* **(d)** *fled the scene, taking Adam with her.*

*C*hoices. We make them every day, often not fully recognizing the impact they have on us as individuals, and on the people around us. Some choices are made for us, but most we make ourselves; and these choices determine the course of our lives. Indeed, it is a sobering thought that our posterity and the very course of history is determined by individual choices.

How much different our lives might be if ordinary individuals had made different choices—right or wrong. These are the infinite *what ifs* of history. Choices that would have significantly changed our heritage.

What if Martin Luther had been persuaded by Pope Leo X to discontinue his protest and abide by the teachings of the church? *What if* Susanna Wesley had chosen not to reconcile with her husband, who had abandoned her, thus precluding the conception of their son John? *What if* Mary Baker Eddy had continued on in the staunch Christian faith of her family and focused her extraordinary energy and abilities on foreign missions? *What if* young, unmarried Maria Anna Schickelgruber had gotten an abortion in 1836 and never given birth to Alois, the father of Adolf Hitler? The list could go on and on.

Or, consider history's two most consequential choices: *What if* Eve had made the right choice when she was tempted by Satan? And *what if* Mary had made the wrong choice when she was confronted with an embarrassing pregnancy? All of history would have to be rewritten.

———

Eve squinted as she opened her eyes, feeling just a twinge of dizziness. The colors and shapes of the flowers and trees, the brightness of the blue sky, the sounds of the birds and insects, and the fragrances—so many different fragrances—almost intoxicated her as they rushed through her virginal senses. For a few moments her world was a glorious kaleidoscope that would not stop turning.

She took a deep breath, pushing the air through her lungs for the first time. Where was she? *Who* was she? What was happening to her? Questions flooded her mind.

Then in her momentary confusion she was startled by a sound. A sound so very different from all the rest. Indeed, it was more than a sound; it was a gentle vibration—a voice that called for a response. She turned, and there he stood, looking at her, his eyes delighting in what he saw. She took her eyes off him and looked at herself. He was like her. They were the same. Yet they were different. His body was taut and muscular; hers was soft and shapely. Each form complemented the other perfectly.

He spoke again, and she understood. He was Adam. She was Eve. His ecstacy could not be contained. "Woman. My equal partner. Bone of my bone and flesh of my flesh!" She infinitely surpassed all of God's magnificent creation. She was far beyond all that he ever could have imagined or dreamed.

They talked. They laughed. They walked through the

garden. Their communion was passionate and deep. They held each other, discovering how their bodies came alive when they touched and caressed and melted together in total oneness.

No worries, no cares, no pressing concerns robbed them of their joyous rapture. Life was perfect. What bliss it was to be alive—to be a woman, to be a man, to be in love. Their hearts were overwhelmed with praise and gratitude and worship. God, in all his wisdom and creative splendor, had allowed them to reflect his glory in human form.

All nature seemed fulfilled, and they were attuned to the creation around them. It was all theirs to enjoy—with one restriction.

Adam explained to Eve that God wanted them to freely eat the delicious fruit from the trees in the garden; he had planted the trees for their pleasure. All but one. God had explicitly instructed Adam not to eat from the Tree of the Knowledge of Good and Evil.

Eve accepted Adam's warning. In fact, it almost seemed trivial. She would never want to displease Adam, let alone God.

But there was someone in the Garden of Eden who was not pleased with God's perfect creation, and he was bent on destroying it. Satan disguised as the serpent.

Eve would be his target, he decided. After all, she had not even been created when God gave Adam the instructions about the tree. He would make her question Adam's word by causing her to doubt that God had actually given him such instructions. It was a clever plan.

Satan found them together in the garden, where he addressed his question to Eve.

"Did God really say, 'You must not eat from any tree in the garden'?" he asked her skeptically.

Eve explained that the ban only involved one tree, and they would die if they even touched it.

"Not so," Satan told her cynically. Not only would they live if they ate that fruit, but they would gain the wisdom of God.

Could this really be true? Eve wondered. If so, it could open up a whole new realm of possibilities. The temptation was agonizing. She loved Adam and wanted to please him. How much more attractive she would be with this infinite wisdom; and he would be equally wise. Together there would be no limit to what they could accomplish.

Adam was silent. Did that mean he would support her decision and go along with her? He wasn't protesting. Surely if Adam were absolutely certain that Satan was wrong he would say so.

The serpent was persistent, holding out the fruit. The urge was powerful. The choice was hers.

She took the fruit. Then she hesitated. No, she wouldn't do it. This creature was trying to deceive her and turn her away from the one who had created her. She threw down the fruit, and she and Adam fled from the presence of the evil intruder.

Eve's heart was pounding. They had escaped the clutches of Satan—but just barely. She felt devastated. How could she have been so tempted? And why did Adam not come to her aid? Together they recognized their vulnerability and vowed that they would abide by God's law.

The sky seemed even bluer and the sun shone more brightly than ever that day. And in the days that followed Eve gave birth to beautiful babies, and the Eden family prospered in their lush surroundings. No sickness, no sadness, no death.

———

Mary was greatly troubled. She was a virgin. She had never had sexual relations with anyone. How could she possibly be pregnant? And what would Joseph think? Her fiancé was a kind and mild-mannered man, but he would certainly never marry her now. And she loved him so much. She couldn't bear the thought of losing him.

What was it the angel had said? That hers was a supernatural pregnancy by the Holy Spirit? But it seemed so utterly preposterous. Surely she must have been dreaming. She buried her face in her hands and wept. "Why is this happening to me? What have I done to deserve this?"

It was an impossible situation, and there was nobody she could talk to. Her mother was a saintly woman, but she would never understand. Her father would be devastated. She didn't even dare tell her best friend. Where could she possibly go for advice? Who could help her out of this awful predicament?

In her despair, Mary thought of the woman who lived near the market at the edge of town. She had a bad reputation, and people avoided being seen with her. The boys told jokes about her, and Mary's girlfriends whispered terrible things about her. They said that men paid money to have sex with her and that women paid her money so that they wouldn't have babies. . . .

It was dark and everyone was asleep when Mary slipped out of the house. Occasionally a dog barked, but otherwise the streets of Nazareth were quiet. Mary saw a lamp flickering in the window as she neared the woman's house. She was afraid. What if the woman had a visitor? What if she got angry and screamed and woke the neighbors? Mary hesitated before the door of the house. Her heart was pounding and her head was spinning. She knew what she was doing was wrong, but she had no other choice. This was her only way out.

When Mary knocked, she was greeted by a gentle voice that invited her into a tiny room lit only by the flickering lamp in the window. Mary was silent, her eyes fastened to the floor. Then she began sobbing. The woman waited patiently for the sobs to subside.

"I'm going to have a baby," Mary whispered at last.

The woman took her hand and squeezed it tightly as Mary poured out her heart about her deep love for Joseph and her fear that she would lose him. The woman understood. Mary agreed to come back the following night. . . .

It was pouring rain the next night as Mary hurried through the dark streets. Her body was tense and her head was throbbing. Oh, if only a bolt of lightning would strike her dead, how much easier it would be. But she was convinced this was the only choice she had; and the woman would keep her secret. The coins weighed heavily in her pocket as she knocked at the door. Mary entered and followed the woman into the back room. . . .

Mary's mother was distressed the next morning to find her daughter feverish and ill. She gently swabbed her face and neck with cool, wet towels, wishing her husband had not already left for the fields. For three days her daughter slipped in and out of consciousness as the fever raged. Then it subsided and Mary slowly regained her strength. Her family was greatly relieved by her physical recovery, but they were concerned. Mary was just not the same. She didn't smile and laugh as she used to; her cheery disposition was gone. Joseph noticed it, too. He tried to tell her how much he cared for her, but she offered little response. Yet he was pleased that she had recovered enough to carry on with their wedding plans.

After the wedding Mary and Joseph began to adjust to the routine of married life. That daily humdrum was broken, however, when they received notice that they were to go to Bethlehem to pay their taxes. They set off, as did many of their neighbors, by foot and by donkey over the dusty roads to the south. It was late when they arrived in Bethlehem, and the town was crowded with other taxpayers.

Joseph managed to secure accommodations for the night in an animal shelter behind one of the local inns. There they found a spot in a corner on some dry hay and lay down, exhausted from the journey.

But Mary couldn't sleep. She tossed and turned. Finally she arose and walked over to the open door. There were stars in the night sky—ordinary stars, nothing unusual. And there were shepherds out in the field some distance away, barely visible in the moonlight. They were watching their sheep as they normally did.

Mary reflected on the months that had passed. This was just about the time when her little one would have been born. She stroked her abdomen and thought of what might have been. She looked back at Joseph sleeping in the hay. He was a good man. She began to weep softly, pondering in her heart what she had done. Her muffled sobs broke the stillness. Otherwise, it was a silent night in Bethlehem.

———

These two "what if" scenarios reveal the incredible potential our choices have for good or for evil and how important it is to choose wisely. Eve made a wrong choice with far-reaching consequences. Mary made a right one. But let's not confuse the choices with the women themselves. Eve is not the epitome of evil, as she has often been portrayed, and Mary is not the epitome of perfection.

Eve and Mary, the first ladies of the Old and New Testaments, are larger-than-life figures. Their names are known even by people who know virtually nothing about the Bible. They have become prototypes of womanhood in all generations; indeed, the church itself through the centuries has interpreted the essence of womanhood through the models of Eve and Mary.

When we think of Eve and Mary, we often think of them as opposites. This was brought home to me recently when I heard a professor ask his students to name the "good" women and the "bad" women in the Bible. Apart from my suspicions about the validity of the exercise, I was uneasy when Mary was immediately placed on the "good" list, and Eve quickly found her way to the "bad."

But when we reflect on Eve and Mary, we begin to see that their differences were not as great as their similarities. Both had crucial roles to fulfill and choices to make. Both had the potential of failing and frustrating God's highest purpose. Eve could have chosen to rebuke Satan and continue to enjoy perfect harmony with God and nature. But, of course, the Bible tells a very different story. What went wrong? What psychological and spiritual tools might Eve have employed to avoid making the wrong choice?

Like Eve, Mary could have made the wrong choice. (Of course, if Eve had made the right choice, Mary's choice would never have been necessary.) That Mary even entertained the thought of having an abortion is highly unlikely, but certainly that would be one of the options facing a woman in like circumstances today. What prepared Mary to make the right choice? What inner strength and spiritual qualities prompted her obedient response to God? And what can we learn from the very opposite responses of these two women?

First we must discard the misleading portrayals we have of them—portrayals that depict Mary embodying everything that is good in womanhood and Eve embodying all that is bad. Mary is compliant and pure; Eve is conniving and evil.

Ben Sira, a rabbi living some two centuries before Jesus, represented the Jewish thought of his day when he wrote: "From a woman did sin originate, and because of her we all must die." Early Christian thinkers made similar statements, sometimes malevolent in nature. Tertullian, a church father of the early third century, saw Eve in all women: "Woman, you are the devil's doorway. You have led astray one whom the devil would not dare attack directly. It is your fault that the Son of God had to die; you should always go in mourning and rags." St. Ambrose, a fourth-century theologian, wrote: "Adam was led to sin by Eve and not Eve by Adam. It is just and right that woman accept as lord and master him whom she led to sin."[1]

Mary has also been distorted by theologians, particularly by Roman Catholics during the Middle Ages and in the centuries following. Thomas Aquinas summed up the most commonly held view: "As a virgin she was conceived, as a virgin gave birth, and she remains a virgin forever." Today, in some areas of the world, Mary has become a virtual god.

Protestants have never claimed sinlessness for Mary— not quite, but almost. She is considered a model of purity and submissiveness, and according to Charles Ryrie her life offers lessons "mostly related to the home." James Hastings enlarges on that idea: "Mary was of a retiring nature, unobtrusive, reticent, perhaps even shrinking from observation, so that the impress of her personality was confined to the sweet sanctities of the home circle. . . . We see in the little that is told of her what a true woman ought to be."[2]

But does the Bible actually portray Mary in this light? Do we really find her in the home, shrinking from observation? When we look closely at the biblical account, we rarely find Mary at home. She is always on the move, whether visiting Elizabeth or going to Bethlehem, or fleeing to Egypt, or making a pilgrimage to Jerusalem for the Passover.

Both Eve and Mary have been refashioned by Bible teachers and theologians, and we must be on guard so that we do not substitute opinion and speculative analysis for the biblical record. Eve and Mary are the perfect candidates for polar opposites: Eve made a choice that led to the Fall; Mary made a choice that led to Christ's redemption of sinners.

But carrying the contrast beyond the biblical record is a disservice not only to Eve and Mary, but to women of all generations.

The primary difference between Eve and Mary relates to their choices and how those choices affected generations to come. This is the real issue—far more than any inherent badness or goodness of these two women. (Indeed, it was Eve who was created "good," not Mary, who, like the rest of us, was born in sin.) While it is true that none of us will ever be required to make such consequential choices as they did, our choices, like theirs, affect far more than merely ourselves and those around us. Our choices have enduring qualities that pass on from one generation to the next.

We know from Exodus 20:5 (KJV), that God is "a jealous God, visiting the iniquity of the fathers upon the children unto the third and fourth generation," and that is certainly true for the sins of the mothers as well. And not just biological mothers. As a teacher and writer, I must be ever watchful of what I pass on to others. I must never forget that my words and my example will have a rippling effect for generations to come.

My choices define me and they are part of what collectively defines Christianity in this generation and generations to follow. I do not speak or act simply for myself, but for all Christians. Jean-Paul Sartre, though not a follower of Christ, made this point, asserting that "when a man commits himself to anything . . . he is not only choosing what he will be, but is thereby at the same time a legislator deciding for the whole of mankind." He offered a challenge that ought to confront us as Christians: "one ought always to ask oneself what would happen if everyone did as one is doing."[3] In other words, what if all Christians made the same kind of choices that I am making? Are my choices ones that reflect positively on Jesus Christ?

I am reminded of Corrie ten Boom and how her choices

have reflected on Christ and how she was so deeply affected by the choices her father made, and he in turn by the choices of his father. Corrie, whose story is told in *The Hiding Place*, was one of four children born into a devout Dutch Reformed family, who for generations had owned and operated a watch shop in the lower level of their home in the town of Haarlem, in the Netherlands. Business contacts with Jewish suppliers in Germany had alerted them to dangers of Nazism long before World War II broke out. They were deeply troubled by the reports, but what could they possibly do to make a difference?

The easy choice would have been the safe choice—to look out for their own needs. But despite the risks, Corrie's father made a very conscious choice to open his home as a sanctuary for hunted Jews.

His was not the first generation of ten Booms to demonstrate concern for Jews. In 1844, Corrie's grandfather started a prayer meeting for the specific purpose of praying for Jewish people, and this concern deepened as the decades passed. Amazingly, it was exactly one hundred years later, in 1944, that the ten Boom home was raided by the Gestapo. Corrie and her father and sister were arrested, but miraculously the Jewish fugitives were so well hidden in their home that they eluded the authorities.

The months that followed that cold February morning were filled with terror. Corrie and her sister Betsy were incarcerated at Ravensbruck, a notorious women's death camp, while their father languished in a prison cell. In May, they received word that he had died.

The conditions at Ravensbruck were appalling—long hours of forced labor, rat-infested unheated barracks, disease, malnutrition, and physical abuse. Yet, during their imprisonment, Corrie and Betsy were able to reach out in love to the ravaged women around them and encourage them to put their trust in God. At night they would huddle together and read the Bible and pray that they would be released. Betsy was released, but only through death. She died on Christmas Day, 1944. Corrie was released soon after—due to a "clerical error." Later she learned that the other women in her age group had been put to death the following week.

The suffering the ten Boom family endured was not in vain. Corrie's story inspired millions of people as she traveled to sixty-four countries during her thirty-three years of public ministry. On one occasion she spoke at a prison filled with hardened criminals. There she told them how her sister Nollie had written to two Dutchmen who were on trial after the war for betraying her family to the Nazis. Nollie wanted to assure them that she and Corrie, through Christ's example, had forgiven them. Both responded, one to say that her letter had brought him to faith in Christ, the other to say that he regretted she and Corrie had not perished with the others.

Corrie reminded the prisoners that they, too, had a choice to make. Would they accept Christ's forgiveness, or would they harden their hearts before God? Many did accept Christ's forgiveness.

Corrie's faithfulness to God did not arise out of a vacuum. She inherited choices that had been made before she was even born—choices that set the stage for her own life of service. After her terrible suffering in a Nazi death camp, we would understand if she had chosen a life of quiet anonymity or even a life devoted to hunting down her Nazi tormentors. But instead, she chose to devote her life to a ministry of carrying the gospel around the globe—and right back to the German camp where she was incarcerated. Today her legacy lives on in the children and grandchildren and great grandchildren of those her message touched.

What was Corrie's secret? How can we make choices

that will endure from generation to generation? In many respects, the stories of Eve and Mary hold the keys.

Eve and Mary are models for us today because they were women who had much in common with each other and with us. Through their differences—which lie not so much in their "goodness" or "badness" as in how they responded at critical junctures in their lives—we can derive principles for our own decision making.

First of all, when confronted with options, we must remember that we can all be "deceived by the serpent's cunning." Whether through the materialism and secularism of our society, or simply through personal pride and greed, we are often "led astray from . . . sincere and pure devotion to Christ" (2 Cor. 11:3).

Second, when making choices we must keep God in proper focus. This can be summed up in the balance and descending order of that shopworn little triad: God—Others—Self. When that order is reversed or rearranged, our choices betray the distortion.

After she received the news of her supernatural pregnancy, Mary's focus was on God. Not as an afterthought or a "Praise the Lord. Now let's get on with what's important," but at the very center of her thoughts. Indeed, there is not even a hint that she was concerned about her own potential embarrassment (self) or Joseph's predicament (others). Her response to the angel was straightforward: "May it be to me as you have said" (Luke 1:38). Her song, which follows that response, is one that ought to permeate our own outlook on life: "My soul praises the LORD and my spirit rejoices in God my Savior . . . for the Mighty One has done great things for me—holy is his name" (1:46, 49).

In contrast, Eve's focus was not on God but on Satan. She certainly had an awareness of God as she conversed with Satan, but she let God be pushed aside. When she listened to Satan's apparently logical questions and answers, he became the "Mighty One" in her eyes. Her perspective became distorted, and she saw herself not as a lowly servant, but as one who could be equal to God. Consequently she made the wrong choice.

The stories of Eve and Mary may seem a bit remote to most of us, but the underlying issue is the very one we struggle with today: What is our focus? Are we serving God or Satan?

God-conscious choices flow naturally out of a God-conscious life, but that does not occur automatically. Like Mary, we must be prepared. Her response to the angel's message and her song to God did not arise out of a vacuum. She was very much aware of who was the center of her thoughts.

Yet while Mary's choice was a God-conscious one, it did not ignore others and self. Her decision would have far-reaching consequences for others—a critical factor she recognized and could not lightly dismiss. "From now on *all generations* will call me blessed," she prophesied (Luke 1:48, italics mine).

Whether Eve realized how profoundly her decision would affect all generations is not revealed in Scripture, but there is no evidence that the thought even entered her mind. Our choices do affect others—those around us and those in generations to come. God *and* others must figure in the choices we make.

So must self. It may seem superfluous to suggest this, since self is often the *only* factor we consider, or at least the overriding factor. But denying or ignoring self can be equally detrimental to decision making.

Mary was *self*-conscious when she faced the ultimate choice in her life. She knew who she was and what her relationship was to God. She was his "servant," and a lowly servant at that. But there was no low self-esteem here; indeed, there is every indication that Mary had a healthy self-image. How else could she say with such certainty that generations would call her *blessed*? She was an unwed, pregnant teenager who might have been stooped in shame, but she held her head high, knowing that she reflected the image of God.

For Eve, *self* was an overriding concern. She was seeking pleasure and self-promotion, good food and wisdom. Although she seemed to recognize God's authority, she never acknowledged her own servant status. Eve was created in the image of God—a perfect human being—and yet she apparently was not satisfied. And by reversing the triad— God, Others, Self—she made a wrong choice. A very wrong choice.

Despite this, we must underscore that we cannot call Eve "bad" and Mary "good," inferring that bad women make bad choices and good women make good choices. Even good women make bad choices. "Just as Eve was deceived by the serpent's cunning," we are all "led astray" sometimes from our "sincere and pure devotion to Christ" (2 Cor. 11:3). Today, perhaps even more than in generations past, women have tough choices to make, and the issues are not easily categorized as *good* and *bad*, traditionalist or feminist, homemaker or working mother.

The issue is decision making, and we as women, like Eve and Mary, have much more in common than we often suppose. We can look to Mary for right principles for right choices, but we must not fail to look at Eve and recognize our own vulnerabilities. In both of them we are reminded how consequential their choices were in generations past and how consequential our choices are for generations to come.

Future generations will look back on us—even as we look back on Eve and Mary and Corrie ten Boom. Will their lives be richer and fuller and more Christ honoring as a result of the choices we have made? Will our children and our children's children be able to stand securely on our shoulders? Will our lives serve as a bridge as they seek richer ground in the journey of life?

The past had its moment; we have ours. . . . We are like soldier ants, moving from a depleted area to seek food beyond, in an unexplored terrain. We have encountered a river that separates us from sight of the future; we have a choice only to die where we stand, or to enter it. The ants always enter and drown. They drown by the millions, and in their death add their bodies to a bridge on which the survivors can cross to what they hope will be richer ground.

—*Marilyn French*
Beyond Power, *1985*

Three

Spiritual Choices

Ruth's choice to cling to her mother-in-law, Naomi, and to
return to her homeland and live and worship with her people
indicates: **(a)** *a deep love and respect for her mother-in-law,* **(b)**
lack of independent thinking, **(c)** *a profound desire to find and*
know God, **(d)** *God's sovereign control over her life.*

*W*hen *I was growing up* in a little country church in the
1950s, I learned Bible stories on flannelgraph. From the
Creation to the conversion of Paul, biblical truths came alive
when my Sunday school teacher rearranged paper figures on
painted flannel backgrounds. The story of Ruth was easy,
not nearly as complicated as King Saul and David, or Elisha
and Elijah. We started out with four people—Naomi,
Elimelech, and their two sons—on the road to Moab to
escape famine. It never took them long to get to the other
side of the flannel board; and once there, the foursome was
suddenly minus one when Elimelech died of unknown
causes. Then two female figures were added, with the
marriage of Naomi's two sons to Orpah and Ruth. (We
never had to memorize the names of the sons—and perhaps
for good reason: this story was about women.)

   Ten years flew by quickly, and the sons died and joined
their father in flannelgraph heaven. Now the family was
down to three, and they were on the road again, this time in
the reverse direction, back to Judah. But before they got
very far, Naomi had second thoughts about this arrangement and urged her daughters-in-law to return to their

"mother's home," perhaps indicating their own fathers were dead also. After considerable deliberation, Orpah reluctantly returned to her people; but Ruth continued on the road with Naomi, and together they ended up back on the side of the flannel board where it all began.

How am I to judge Ruth, that Old Testament saint for whom I was named? And how can she even in a remote sense serve as a role model for women today? In many respects this Moabite widow seems less than noble to me. Her decision to adopt the religion of the Hebrews placed her in the genealogical line of the Messiah, but the nature of that decision does not correspond with my concept of conversion. If I had fashioned her character, I would have brought her through a grueling ordeal of forsaking the decadent deities of Moab; only after a long, hard struggle would she fall to her knees in tears of repentance, pleading for God's forgiveness for worshiping at the altars of Baal.

The Bible, however, offers no such portrait of Ruth. Indeed, her decision to follow the God of Israel could easily be missed by a speed-reader and seems altogether too anticlimatic for a modern-day evangelical. She is simply a loyal and faithful daughter-in-law who dutifully follows Naomi back to her homeland and seems to get religion as part of the package: "Whither thou goest, I will go; and where thou lodgest, I will lodge; thy people shall be my people, and thy God my God" (Ruth 1:16 KJV). Those lines may be fine for a marriage ceremony, but that is not the way conversion is supposed to be—at least not in my religious upbringing, replete with prolonged altar calls and camp-fire commitments. Yet Ruth's choice was a momentous one, and it surely was the right one.

How did she arrive at that decision? Did the Lord "speak" to her? Did he "call" her? Did she pray about it? The Bible gives no indication of any input from God in Ruth's crucial decision—at a time in history when God was certainly on speaking terms with his people. Nevertheless, she stands as a remarkable example of the kind of spiritual choices that begin and sustain our Christian life.

Although some people can testify to profound conversion experiences that have no links to family or friends, most of us came to faith through the influence of others— through the witness and example of a parent or a pastor or perhaps a roommate. And so it was with Ruth. She came into the kingdom holding her mother-in-law's hand. God was not silent. He was speaking loudly and clearly through his servant Naomi. God came to Ruth naturally and supernaturally, and the same can be said as she sought God's continued unfolding of his plan. It came to her naturally, through customs, culture, common sense, circumstances, and family relationships—and a strong dose of God-given resourcefulness on the part of both Naomi and Ruth.

Spiritual choices are often matter-of-fact choices. Yet we resist the idea of simplicity in spiritual matters, especially ones as momentous as conversion, because somehow we think they are supposed to be pious and mystical and maybe climactic.

Some will argue that all choices are spiritual choices. Perhaps so. Certainly there should be a spiritual dimension to all aspects of our life. Too often we compartmentalize life into sacred and secular—and never the twain shall meet. The other extreme, however, is to force everything into a spiritual category. And if everything is spiritual, it is all too easy for nothing to be spiritual.

The most radical spiritual decision a person ever makes, of course, is the decision to follow Christ—or not to follow Christ. The choice is explicit and unmistakable, even as it was for the people of ancient Israel when Joshua put the challenge before them: "Choose for yourselves this day whom you will serve, whether the gods your forefathers served beyond the River, or the gods of the Amorites, in whose land you are living. But as for me and my household, we will serve the Lord" (Josh. 24:15).

Today, perhaps more than any other time in history, the concept of conversion and commitment to biblical faith is being challenged. Dogmatism is out; religious pluralism is in. All religions are good, and all religions lead to God—or so the argument goes. Jesus is not unique; he is only "one Christ" out of many, and Christianity is just one option in a smorgasbord of religious pluralism. There are no absolutes, no objective standards. "Your truth is your truth; my truth is my truth." The New Age movement and the mentality that goes along with it has left this indelible stamp on our generation.

But even before the heresy of New Age there was the "heresy" of privatized religion, which says, "Faith is a *personal* choice." Now it is true that faith is a personal choice, a commitment to God by an individual. But this is only one side of the coin. Faith is also corporate. We are incubated in the faith by the warmth of family and friends, and without those continued relationships our faith is at risk.

Ruth's conversion was not simply a private, individual matter. Her decision was directly related to her relationship with Naomi. Her faith was personal but it was also corporate, and her commitment to the God of Israel was as natural as her commitment to her mother-in-law. Likewise, God has given *us* relationships with others, and those relationships should serve us in coming to God and in bringing others into the kingdom.

Although I was led to believe that my decision, at the age of seven, to follow Jesus was a private one, I know now it was not. Miss Buck, a Bible college student who gave a week of her summer to teach vacation Bible school in rural Wisconsin, took me by the hand and became my Naomi. And three decades later when my son decided to follow

Jesus, I reached down and took him by the hand and helped to bring him into the kingdom. And so it goes, from friend to friend and generation to generation.

Yet our evangelistic style is so often simplified by shortcuts. How blithely we talk about "sharing" our faith, when in reality all we do is leave it on the doorstep, ring the bell, and run. "Sharing" is an exercise that involves time and interaction. I think back to my college years when I stalked the beach during vacation break with "The Four Spiritual Laws." I will never forget a stringy-haired teenage girl I encountered in Lake George, New York. I caught up with her as she was making her way from the beach to the parking lot, and she seemed appreciative that I took the time to talk to her. Right there on the sidewalk she made a profession of faith—and then walked out of my life. For my part—to mix metaphors—it was hit and run and another notch on my gun. If her commitment was more than a momentary whim, if she did go on in the faith, it was in spite of any role I played.

It is interesting to note that the Bible does not give any indication that Orpah, Naomi's other daughter-in-law, contemplated forsaking her pagan idols to worship the God of Israel. Nor is there any indication that Naomi challenged her to do so. Naomi's faith was part of her way of life, and when Ruth joined her on the road from Moab to Judah, she joined her in that journey of faith.

We must embrace the truth that this most momentous spiritual choice in life is both vertical and horizontal, and it is the horizontal aspect of our commitment to God that helps secure the staying power of our faith. I would not even want to hazard a guess at how many children have made professions of faith in backyard Bible clubs or church outreach programs only to be left without nourishment to die on the vine. What a tragedy. Faith in God is not a solitary venture. It is a journey from Moab to Judah that requires the companionship of corporate faith.

Horizontal relationships are necessary to sustain us through the ups and downs of a lifetime of faith. When we sometimes endure what seems to be a deafening silence on the part of God, we need to hear reassuring voices of corporate faith. When we shout at God amid our grief and pain and all we hear is the angry echo of our own screams, we need corporate faith. And when we turn so far away from God in doubt and indifference that we don't even bother to shout, we need corporate faith. When our faith fails and we can no longer walk without stumbling, we need to lean on others who serve as our crutches until our faith can once again sustain us.

But corporate faith must not be confused with five nights a week in church fellowship. Rather, it is a strong support system that encourages us to seek discernment and shun overdependency. Ultimately our choices are ours, and ours alone, to make.

For this and other reasons, corporate faith is not enough. Making right spiritual choices also depends on the nourishment of the soul that only comes through solitude—a priceless commodity we often take for granted or avoid. The early Christian saints who went out into the desert searching for spirituality through silence and solitude were guilty of excess, but they recognized the value of drawing on resources from deep within the soul.

"It is a difficult lesson to learn today—to leave one's friends and family and deliberately practice the art of solitude for an hour or a day or a week," writes Anne Morrow Lindbergh in *Gift from the Sea*. "There is a quality to being alone that is incredibly precious. . . . Every person, especially every woman, should be alone sometime during the year; some part of each week, and each day."[1]

Sometimes we can find solitude in the midst of noise and

commotion. I recall the summers during my high school years when I worked in a canning factory. My job was to pick leaves and stems off of the beans as they went by on a conveyor. There were people all around me, but it was too noisy to talk, so I was in my own world—my world of solitude. It was there my imagination flourished and dreams were born. And it was there I could talk to God uninterrupted and draw from inner resources that had been stored for just such a time.

When we think of times of solitude and communion with God, the term *prayer* naturally comes to mind. Prayer is a major theme of Scripture and ought to be a major theme of every Christian's life. But prayer is much easier to talk about than it is to do; and when it is talked about, prayer is too often demeaned. God is treated like a rich grandfather up in the sky who gives us whatever we want whenever we ask. He is, of course, much greater than we are, but in our minds he's there primarily to do our bidding.

This is the message we hear from the health-and-wealth preachers who sound like modern-day versions of Charles Fillmore, the nineteenth century cult leader who proclaimed to his followers: "You cannot *use* God too often. He loves to be *used*, and the more you *use* Him the more easily you *use* Him and the more pleasant His help becomes."[2]

Another concept of prayer comes from Perky Brandt in her book *Two Way Prayer*. She believes that just as we talk to God, so God talks to us, and through such communication we can discern God's will on issues ranging from health matters to building a new church sanctuary. If we are not receiving such messages, we are not listening. It's as simple as that—though listening is a consciously learned process.[3]

My own heritage, the weekly prayer meeting, offered another variation. After a perfunctory time of praise and thanksgiving, we recited our "prayer requests." We always laid out our specific plans or needs to God, then let the matter rest with, "Thy will—not mine—be done, O Lord." It was certainly a convenient way to evade any concerns about "unanswered" prayer.

Unfortunately none of the above truly get to the heart of prayer. They all focus on what we *get* from God. Prayer is communion with God—not so much in the words we say as in the expression that comes from our hearts. If it were just the words, many of us would be considered professionals. Think of how often we hear people who pray well. I confess, not proudly but honestly, that I pray well. Ask me on a moment's notice to lead the adult Sunday school class in opening prayer, and I can get to my feet and sound like I'd been rehearsing all Saturday night. But is that what constitutes communion with God? I don't think so. I don't deny the validity of public prayer, but knowing my own ability, contrasted with what I know can be in my heart, I'm often skeptical of the high-sounding phrase.

Prayer can also be manipulative. I recently received a phone call asking me to pray about some needed funds, but quickly sensed that it was really more of a request for funds from me than a request for prayer. On the other hand, people do use prayer as an excuse not to get involved. How easy it is to just pray for the widow who can't meet the mortgage payment when we ourselves have the capability to answer that prayer. And when someone asks us to help out with vacation Bible school, we say "I'll pray about it," which puts the blame squarely on God if *we* decide not to do it.

Prayer can even serve as a sewer line for gossip. Have you ever said—or had someone say to you—in a low, spiritual whisper, "We really need to pray for Jennifer. She was caught shoplifting, you know." Gossip is bad enough, but it borders on blasphemy when we try to spiritualize it by turning prayer into an occasion for a sanctimonious exchange of information.

The fact is, these kinds of prayer can be dangerous to

our health—our spiritual health at least. Should we then quit praying? God forbid! What we need is a perspective on prayer that does not allow for manipulation of God or of each other.

When I think of true prayer, I think of the old hymn, "In the Garden." It was my mother's favorite hymn. We sang it at her funeral, and even after more than twenty years, I still sometimes choke up when I sing it. It's a hymn of prayer that powerfully portrays the kind of communion we ought to have with God: intimate prayer with no set place or agenda and no time clock. The garden might be our bedroom or breakfast nook, or it may be our backyard, "while the dew is still on the roses." But most of all, the garden is in our hearts, where the deepest expression of intimacy flows.

> *I come to the garden alone,*
> *While the dew is still on the roses;*
> *And the voice I hear, falling on my ear,*
> *The Son of God discloses.*
>
> *And He walks with me, and He talks with me,*
> *And He tells me I am His own,*
> *And the joy we share as we tarry there,*
> *None other has ever known.*

The communion pictured here is intimate friendship, not a set recitation of appropriate pious platitudes. Imagine having your closest friend always address you in the same formal (or informal), predictable routine. Would that foster intimacy? Surely not. The same is true with God. Through our prayers we come to *know* God, and through knowing God we discern his will.

Knowing God through prayer is beautifully illustrated by the testimony of Kari Torjesen Malcolm. Raised in China, the daughter of Norwegian missionaries, Kari suddenly found her life put on hold by World War II. Her father was killed by the enemy, and Kari, a teenager, was held for three years in a Chinese concentration camp, along with many of her classmates.

"Our homes had been confiscated, and our bank accounts closed," she writes. "Gone were all the things we thought were our birthright: our education, three square meals a day and our privacy. Even our beds were gone. Our world had been reduced to a space on the floor of a room. The enemy had taken everything and given us a wall with electrified barbed wire and a deep moat."

Kari had come to faith in Christ as a child through the testimony and example of her parents, but while she was in the concentration camp she lost the sense of security she had known. Identified by her captors simply as "number 16," her very identity eroded.

"It was during our second year in prison camp that my good friend Debbie decided to organize a prayer group," Kari recalls. "Some of us teen-agers who had gone to school together before internment got permission from the guards to climb the bell tower every day at noon for our rendezvous. As we met to pray, only one type of prayer was voiced, 'Lord, get us out of here!'"

Those times of prayer brought a sense of community to the students, but for Kari they also brought a sense of emptiness. Were their prayers a waste of time? Was there really a God at all?

Struggling with her doubts, Kari pleaded with God to reveal himself to her, and God did.

First of all she came to the realization that God was all she really possessed. The enemy had taken her father and her freedom, "but the one thing they could not touch was my relationship to my God." At that point the prayers for freedom no longer seemed relevant to Kari. "There was more to life than just getting out of prison," she says. With that new perspective, she decided one day not to join the others for the noon prayer time. What followed changed her life:

> Debbie looked for me right after the meeting. The spot where we met is riveted in my memory. I cannot even remember trying to defend myself, but Debbie must have surmised something of what had occurred in my thinking. Her reproof ended with a final taunt, "So we aren't good enough for you anymore, eh? Getting holier than the rest of us, I can see."
>
> As I walked away, I felt lonelier than I had ever felt in my life. My last bit of security was peeled off. This was the climax to the peeling process that had been going on through the war years with the loss of my father, my home, my education, my freedom. Now I no longer belonged to my peer group.
>
> It was only then that I was able to pray the prayer that changed my life: "Lord, I am willing to stay in this prison for the rest of my life if only I may know you." At that moment I was free.[4]

Following the war and her return to freedom, Kari's continuing desire to know God assisted her in making the right choices that unfolded as the will of God for her life. After graduating from Wheaton College, she married an American, and she and her husband served as missionaries for many years in the Philippines. Kari admits that her relationship with God has had its ups and downs, but her desperate desire to *know* him, born in that prison camp, has not left her.

If we are to make right choices, we must know God: We must walk with him and talk with him, as the old hymn reminds us; we must take one step at a time as his will for us unfolds.

Perhaps it was that way for Ruth as she gleaned behind the workmen in the field, contemplating all that had transpired since she left Moab, speculating about what the future held for her.

To some, Ruth's manner of finding God's will after she

arrived in Judah may be more troublesome than her seemingly lackluster conversion. From our perspective she and Naomi appear to be conniving women as they set out to snare Boaz as a husband for Ruth. Yet this process was entirely consistent with the culture and customs of the day, and through it God revealed his ideal choice for Ruth.

Misconceptions about "finding the will of God for our lives" have led some to assume that God's will is something he reveals to us in some mystical and mysterious way. The story of Ruth, however, portrays God's will as something that unfolds through a lifetime of actively making right choices.

Ruth took an active part in finding God's will when it came to marriage. Such a role is sometimes shunned by Christian women today—at least outwardly—as I have found among those in my course on women in cross-cultural ministry. These young women know all too well that a career in missions limits their prospects for marriage. They desire marriage, yet do not want to admit that they could take active steps in bringing that about. The only spiritual option is to pray. Any kind of overt activity on their part would be potentially interfering with God's will, so the argument goes.

But just think about this in regard to some of the day-to-day concerns in our lives. If we are looking for a better job or an apartment closer to work, do we do nothing but pray? Even the most spiritual among us would also be developing a course of action to achieve our goals—looking through the want ads, making phone calls, arranging interviews. Would it be just as appropriate to develop a course of action in seeking a prospective marriage partner, as Ruth did, but within our own cultural norms?

The "call" of God is another aspect of finding the will of God. But if the call were a written command signed and sealed by God Almighty, it would create considerably less confusion for us. It doesn't work that way though. The "call," like that ambiguous chart known as "the will of God for our lives," is not necessarily a momentary breakthrough from God that comes in a complete package.

Routine choices have eternal consequences. Indeed, it is the sum total of our everyday choices—big and little—that encompasses the will of God. The will of God is not a once-for-all revelation. It is not something to be *found*; it is something to be *lived* out, day by day. The will of God progressively unfolds as we weigh one set of options against another and make right choices, guided by the principles found in the Bible. This is the God-given duty that looms before us on our pilgrimage through life—a duty that demands that we seek to truly *know* God.

The Bible offers overriding principles as we seek to understand God's will. Indeed Paul sets forth the essence of the will of God in emphatic terms for every Christian: "It is God's will that you should be holy," or, as I memorized it as a child from the King James Version: "For this is the will of God, even your sanctification" (1 Thess. 4:3). When this admonition becomes a way of life, God's will naturally falls into place.

On a very practical level we can test our spiritual choices by asking ourselves some penetrating questions:

- Do I really *know* God? Have I merely gone through the motions of conversion—perhaps responding to an altar call—or do I daily walk and talk with God?
- Am I recognizing the corporate aspect of my spiritual pilgrimage, not thinking I can go it alone, while at the same time taking time for solitude?
- Are my prayers true communion with God, or do I seek to *use* God for my own benefit and *use* prayer for self-defense or gossip?
- Do I "over-spiritualize" God's involvement in my life, ignoring the fact that he works through ordinary,

mundane circumstances? Do I "under-spiritualize" God by thinking he was on "speaking terms" with people only in Bible times?
• Am I conscious that God's will unfolds through my everyday right choices, but that the ultimate right choice is my sanctification—that I live a holy life?

There's an old hymn that sums up what our attitude ought to be as we contemplate our faith in God and his will for our lives. It is as fresh today as it was when it was written more than a century ago, especially as it relates to spiritual choices.

Take time to be holy, speak oft with the Lord;
    Abide in Him always, and feed on His Word.
Make friends of God's children, help those who are weak,
    Forgetting in nothing, His blessings to seek.

Take time to be holy, the world rushes on;
    Spend much time in secret, with Jesus alone.
By looking to Jesus, like Him you will be;
    Your friends, in your conduct, His likeness shall see.

Take time to be holy, let Him be your guide,
    And run not before him, whatever betide.
In joy or in sorrow, still follow the Lord,
    And, looking to Jesus, still trust in His Word.

Take time to be holy, be calm in your soul—
    Each thought and each motive, beneath His control.
Thus led by His spirit, to fountains of love,
    You soon will be fitted, for service above.
                     —*William D. Longstaff (1822–94)*

Four

Lifestyle Choices

Priscilla's decision to combine menial labor and marriage with ministry and mobility is an illustration of: (a) *a saintly superwoman,* (b) *a first-century feminist,* (c) *a frazzled female frustrated by conflicting choices,* (d) *a fruitful ministry facilitated by a flexible and functional lifestyle.*

Like so many biblical characters, Priscilla suddenly appears in the text minus any personal history—a biographer's nightmare. We can only imagine what sort of a woman she was, and her name offers the first clue. She is most frequently referred to as Priscilla, a nickname of sorts that her friend Paul felt comfortable using. But Paul also addressed her by the more formal variant, Prisca, a name which appears often in Roman inscriptions, leading some to believe that she may have come from a prominent family. If that were true, however, why was she married to a tentmaker, and why was she actively involved in that smelly work herself? Was she a rich girl who ran off with the animal skinner from the other side of the tracks?

Another clue, perhaps the most striking, is the name inversion of Priscilla and Aquila. Paul actually puts Priscilla's name before her husband's, as in Romans 16 where the apostle heads his list of greetings with "Greet Priscilla and Aquila" (Rom. 16:3). No doubt she was a prominent leader in the early church and thus more readily recognized than her husband. Otherwise it is unlikely that Paul would have

57

inverted their names, a conspicuous departure from the convention of placing the husband's name first.

Perhaps Priscilla was more dynamic than her husband; perhaps her ministry was more effective than his. Perhaps she had become a Christian before he did; or perhaps she had more education and social prominence. Whatever the situation, even more significant than their individuality is their togetherness. Priscilla and Aquila are never referred to separately.

Priscilla was a student of the Scriptures as well as a teacher. When the educated Alexandrian Jew, Apollos, came to town and began his fervent preaching in the synagogue, Priscilla and her husband invited him to their home—and not just as a social gesture. Apollos did not have the message quite straight, so "Priscilla and Aquila . . . explained to him the way of God more adequately" (Acts 18:26).

Some even have speculated that Priscilla was the author of the book of Hebrews. There are a number of reasons to draw this conclusion, the most convincing of which is that this lengthy epistle was not signed, as other such letters were. In those days if a woman had written it, she would have had good reason not to put her name on it.

What we know for certain about Priscilla is that she was a cherished coworker of the apostle Paul. She and Aquila were living in Corinth when Paul met them. They had just moved there from Rome, where they had been victims of persecution under Emperor Claudius, who had ordered all Jews out of the city. Being both Christians and tentmakers, they immediately found a common interest with Paul, and apparently the friendship between them quickly blossomed. In fact, Paul stayed on and lived in their home for a year and a half. When the apostle left Corinth, Priscilla and Aquila accompanied him as far as Ephesus; and while Paul traveled on to other cities, they apparently remained there to work and witness.

The ministry in Ephesus was often tension-filled, for this idolatrous city was devoted to the cult of Artemis. After Paul returned there, a riot broke out among those who saw Christianity as a threat to their way of life (Acts 19). The situation was dangerous, and there is reason to believe Paul's life may have been spared by the courageous intervention of Priscilla and Aquila. "They risked their lives for me," he wrote. "Not only I but all the churches of the Gentiles are grateful to them" (Rom. 16:4).

Priscilla and Aquila continued to minister whenever and wherever they were needed; they returned to Rome and then back again to Ephesus, where a congregation of believers worshiped in their home (1 Cor. 16:19). That is the last we hear of them, but tradition (some would say legend) tells us that they were beheaded for the sake of Christ. In the Roman Catholic church their martyrdom is commemorated on July 8.

Priscilla effectively combined her trade of tentmaking with her ministry and her marriage. Apparently she did not consider menial labor beneath her, and she was flexible enough to live a mobile lifestyle that took her wherever the Lord led. Through the choices she made, she created a lifestyle formula that was perfectly suited for her as an individual and perfectly fitted to accomplish God's will for her life.

All of which offers a valuable and relevant lesson for us today. We are not all suited to be a Priscilla, but we are all obligated to make lifestyle choices that fit us best for fulfilling God's will for our lives.

Sometimes I think it would be great if all Christians, at about the age of twenty, could enroll in Lifestyle Choices 101, taught by a godly believer who could present biblical, historical, and contemporary models for each student to consider. It is so easy to spend our time dreaming of the "Lifestyles of the Rich and Famous," while we unconsciously fall into a consumer-oriented way of life. Plans for graduate degrees and career promotions and home ownership take precedence over lifestyle choices suited to our own personalities and to a committed Christian life.

I have friends who are part of JPUSA (Jesus People USA), a Christian ministry in Chicago. They live communally, and, except for small allowances, all earnings go into a common fund. Their lives are devoted to serving others in a way that is unusual in our capitalistic, materialistic society. I admire them tremendously, but their lifestyle is not for everyone. Indeed, JPUSA stands out as one of the few Christian communes that has survived the test of time.

Another person who developed a lifestyle to suit her personality and ministry is Karen Mains, also of Chicago. In her book *Open Heart, Open Home*, she tells about how she, as an inner-city pastor's wife, began to focus on hospitality as her ministry: not to the kind of people who would be able to set a beautiful table and return the invitation, but to those who had no homes or could not afford to provide a meal for guests. Her aim was to focus on individuals, not on waxing the kitchen to a shine or making perfect individual Jell-O molds. It was a lifestyle of *hospitality,* not *entertainment*, and she makes a significant distinction between the two.

> Entertaining says, "I want to impress you with my beautiful home and clever decorating, my gourmet cooking." Hospitality, however, seeks to minister. It says, "This home is not mine. It is truly a gift from my Master. I am his servant and I use it as He desires."[1]

My friends Gretchen and Bob Passantino are a modern-day version of Priscilla and Aquila. They operate a counter-cult and apologetics ministry from their home in Southern California, and together they write books and lecture all over the country on contemporary issues related to spiritual discernment. Then there are Joan and Bud Berends, who were determined that their retirement years would not be spent on the golf course or restaurant hopping to catch the daily senior-citizen lunch specials. They took early retirement in order to serve in medical missions in Kenya, and even sold their beautiful home, realizing, as Bud puts it, that "we didn't own the house; the house owned us."

Lifestyle choices are conscious choices, and they are ones that may very well involve sacrifice.

Paul emphasized the fact that the Christian life ought to be distinctly different. Indeed, in Romans 12:1–2 he cuts right to the heart of this issue when he speaks of sacrifice and nonconformity: "Therefore, I urge you, brothers [and sisters], in view of God's mercy, to offer your bodies as living sacrifices, holy and pleasing to God—which is your spiritual worship. Do not conform any longer to the pattern of this world, but be transformed by the renewing of your mind. Then you will be able to test and approve what God's will is—his good, pleasing and perfect will."

Paul's appeal for us to present our *bodies* as a living sacrifice has relevance to our lifestyle choices today. One such choice that is surfacing as a controversial issue in our church circles is the homosexual lifestyle. It is sometimes assumed that sexual orientation or sexual preference ought to determine lifestyle, but that assumption is not biblical and is being challenged by more and more professionals in the mental health field.

Dr. Elizabeth Moberly is one such professional. She maintains that homosexuality is more a product of the environment than of genetics. But whatever the root causes, she insists that gays and lesbians, like everyone else, have *lifestyle* choices to make. She draws a clear distinction between homosexuality and the homosexual lifestyle, and while the former may not involve any choice on the part of the individual, the latter does: "As an adult, I think that

person has some significant choices: the choice whether to
act that orientation out sexually or not, and the choice
whether or not to seek therapy. Those are significant adult
choices."[2]

Singles are faced with similar lifestyle choices. Do they
act out their sexual desires, or do they stay true to the
scriptural admonition regarding sexual abstinence? It is a
difficult choice for many singles who find themselves in
their twenties or beyond with no prospects for marriage.
Yet Scripture is clear on this point: the only option—as
with homosexuals—is to pursue a full and vibrant lifestyle
minus sexual activity. In this area and in all our lifestyle
choices we can be challenged by the example of others,
especially by those who have carved out unique patterns of
living that suited their personality and gifts and that
enhanced their effectiveness in ministry. Henrietta Mears is
one such individual.

Henrietta Mears, a leading Christian educator a generation ago, made an indelible impression on the lives of a
multitude of young people who went on to become
influential Christian leaders, including Bill Bright and Billy
Graham. Her life spanned seventy-one years, between 1890
and 1961, and her lifestyle uniquely suited her gifts and
personality. Yet it had a timeless, universal quality that
ought to challenge all of us.

Singleness was not a premeditated choice for Henrietta.
She wanted marriage and a family as much as any young
woman. But she was also committed to serving God. And so
on a spring night in Minnesota she found herself faced with
one of the most crucial decisions of her life—one of the
most crucial decisions any woman can make. Would she
choose marriage, or would she choose the freedom her
single life offered her? The young banker she had been
dating had asked her to marry him. He loved her, and he

offered her almost everything she could have asked for, but her answer was no.

When Henrietta turned down his proposal, she was a chemistry teacher in Minnesota. But that was only a means of accomplishing her real purpose: reaching out with the gospel to those who might not otherwise be reached. When the boys in her small-town high school wanted a football team, she organized it and joined them on the muddy field for practice, with the expectation that they would join her later in a Bible study. After she moved to a new position in Minneapolis, she agreed to teach a small Sunday school class of contemptuous teenage girls. Within a few years the class had grown to over five hundred.

Her reputation as a highly effective Christian educator quickly spread, and Henrietta was invited to head the educational program at Hollywood Presbyterian Church in California. It was a mighty challenge. The church was large and affluent—and stuck in a rut in the area of educational ministries. But Henrietta Mears was determined, and within three years she saw the Sunday school enrollment increase from less than five hundred to more than four thousand.

Dissatisfied with existing Sunday school materials, she began developing her own, a venture that soon turned into Gospel Light Publishing Company. She also found time to teach Bible classes, with many famous Hollywood stars among her students. But the most gratifying aspect of her job, and her first love, was the College Department. During her more than thirty years at Hollywood Presbyterian, Henrietta Mears taught thousands of students from UCLA, USC, and other local colleges and universities. She also invited these young people to her home and often counseled late into the night with those who lined up to speak privately with her. More than four hundred of her students went on into full-time ministry.

Henrietta's magnetic personality and flair often caught

people off guard. She dressed to the hilt, with flashy rings, brightly colored dresses, and big hats decked with plumes and flowers—her trademark. She was embarrassed that the "dowdy look" was considered the stamp of a Christian, and she vowed she would do her best to erase that impression.

She also quickly disposed of the myth that Christians were to be meek and mild. Once when she was on tour in India, visiting the Taj Mahal, the guide jumped up on a platform to demonstrate the marvelous acoustics in the building. He shouted out: "There is no God but Allah, and Mohammed is his prophet!" Henrietta asked the guide if she could try out the acoustics herself, and with his permission she shouted, "Jesus Christ, Son of God, is Lord over all."

She was a woman of conviction and never missed an opportunity to prod people along in the Christian life, even if it meant stepping on toes. On one occasion during a testimony time with her college students she became so agitated that she could listen no more:

> This has been the most ridiculous testimony time I think I have ever heard. All we have been talking about is silly little things that don't amount to a hill of beans! Have we lost sight of why we are here? There hasn't been one word about winning the nations for Christ. How about these great campuses in this area? Hasn't anything been done out at UCLA this week? Hasn't anyone witnessed to a student at USC? God weeps over these lost students, and we come here to talk about trifles.[3]

Henrietta was a tireless teacher and evangelist, and when asked how she did it all, she had a blunt reply: "The key is one word—work. Webster spells it, W-O-R-K, and it means just what he says it does. Wishful thinking will never take the place of hard work."[4]

On the other hand, she was no Mother Teresa, whose worn sandals and simple garments blend in well with ghetto life. Nor was she suited to the lifestyle of Jesus People

USA. No, Henrietta went first class. An inheritance allowed her to own a beautiful home, and she was a world traveler, never lacking in personal amenities. With the conviction that all Christians should be able to enjoy at least a little of the good life, she founded Forest Home, a beautiful wooded retreat in nearby San Bernardino.

When asked why she had never married, Henrietta always had a ready answer: "The apostle Paul was born too soon, and I have never found anyone in my generation that could hold a candle to him, but I'll keep looking."[5]

Did she ever regret her single life? Not at all. "The Lord has always given me a beautiful home," she said. "He has given me thousands of children; the Lord has supplied every thing in my life and I've never felt lonely." She insisted that young women should not purposely seek to follow her model of singleness, but she recognized that her own example had made that potential more attractive: "It has pleased me to know that they have been able to see my happiness and my complete satisfaction in the life that the Lord has given me."[6]

Henrietta is a model to us because she was willing to be herself and willing to be different. She did not fit the mold of the world, nor was her lifestyle a clone of other Christian women.

When I think of the variety of lifestyle choices available to women, I sometimes think of my friend Val in Traverse City, Michigan. She's the mother of two teenage boys and has chosen not to work outside the home. Her boys tease her for not working like other moms do, but she is convinced that her full-time career of volunteer work is more important. She is president of Families in Action, a community group for drug and alcohol-free schools, and she's a scout leader, a school library volunteer, and actively involved in her church.

Lifestyle choices are not carved in granite. Henrietta's

lasted a lifetime; others, perhaps like Val, may be appropriate for a shorter length of time. We ought not assume that a particular lifestyle is forever, but be open to new directions that may fit a particular or changing situation.

Recently I saw a Phil Donahue show that featured alternative lifestyles for marriage and family living. The "expert" on the program was Bryan Brook, author of *Design Your Love Life*, a book that offers alternatives for couples who want to preserve the love and fidelity of a traditional marriage but design creative structures to make it work in troublesome situations.[7]

One couple lived in separate rooms under one roof because he was a smoker and she was not. Another couple lived apart three weeks out of the month because the wife's career kept her on the road. Another lived in a house specifically designed for a blended family that could not blend: the wife and her teenage daughters lived in one side of the house with their own kitchen and living room, while the husband and his teenage sons had a similar living arrangement on the other side of the house—with a shared master bedroom in between.

The comments from the audience were mostly negative, and my own initial reaction was one of skepticism. But the more I thought about their situations, the more it seemed as though these couples, by making lifestyle choices that were workable for them, had at least averted divorce—in a society where that seems to be the leading solution when difficulties arise.

Now I'm not advocating these "designer marriages" as an improvement on traditional marriage. Indeed they could well be considered an inferior form of marital lifestyle. But they certainly are better than divorce. From that standpoint, perhaps there ought to be more, not fewer, lifestyle choices today in the realm of marriage and family living.

Some lifestyle choices are as simple as making conscious

decisions on how we spend our leisure time or our discretionary funds. But as simple as these choices may seem, they add up to the sum of our lifestyle—a major element in God's will for our lives.

Many of our choices extend naturally out of our upbringing and personality. For example, I grew up a "country girl," and it seems natural that my lifestyle today includes a lot of outdoor activity—hiking along the Grand River or in nearby parks or forest preserves. Never would I spend a leisure moment in a mall. I go shopping, but to me that is *work*, not pleasure.

Some of my lifestyle choices are more purposeful. When I have a little extra money to spend, it goes for vacation and travel, not furniture and shoes. I place high value on good times and lasting memories. I will forever cherish my Michigan mini-vacations and my five-day February flings in Florida. And these times are not just for me. It's hard to imagine my teenage son looking back one day wishing we'd had better furniture, but I'm already hearing him reminisce with that marvelous opening phrase, "Mom, remember when . . ."

From Priscilla and Henrietta and the other lives we've looked at we can draw a number of principles: in every case the lifestyles reflect sacrifice, commitment, individuality, nonconformity, and outreach.

Henrietta Mears sacrificed a husband and children, but found satisfaction and fulfillment in her commitment and outreach that more than made up for any personal loss. Priscilla ignored first-century decorum that denied a woman an equal place alongside her husband and refused to hide in the background. Nineteen hundred years later that same kind of nonconformity and individuality made Henrietta Mears stand out from the world around her far more than her big hats. She did not let the world "squeeze [her] into its own mold" (Rom. 12:2 PHILLIPS). Rather she caused the world to sit up and take notice of her.

Priscilla was a tentmaker, which at first glance would seem to bear little relevance to our day. In missiological jargon, however, a tentmaker is someone who is first and foremost a missionary but earns a living with another profession (like Priscilla and Aquila and Paul). In modern times this means that secular professions are often the gateway to the mission field, as in the case of an electrical engineer who takes a position in Saudi Arabia for the purpose of reaching the Saudis and others in that part of the world with the gospel. In a very real sense we can all use our jobs and professions and unique talents as stepping-stones to our own mission field, be it a beauty salon or the banking business.

Lifestyle choices ought to be both natural and purposeful—ones that honor God but at the same time fit our own personalities and aspirations. The options are infinite, but the right ones for us become more apparent as we ask ourselves such penetrating questions as:

- Does my lifestyle glorify God? Is it consistent with biblical morality and ethics? Does it demonstrate the uniqueness of the Christian life?

- Does my lifestyle have an outward focus—a natural means of serving others and identifying with their needs? Am I willing to sacrifice my time and material wealth for the benefit of others?

- Is my lifestyle suited to me and to my temperament? Do I find it fulfilling, or have I adopted it to impress others or God?

- Have I explored a variety of options? Have I attended missions fairs, read biographies, visited local ministries, sent away for brochures and information, or talked to friends and acquaintances about alternatives?

- Am I willing to take risks? Am I willing to be just a little bit crazy for God, if that's what it takes?
- Am I conscious of eternal values and what influence my lifestyle has on my immediate family and friends?

Our lifestyles change as we make the choices that confront us and move from one stage to another, but at every stage our lives must be lived according to eternal values, reflecting the image of God to the world around us.

How then shall we live? With eternity ever in view, but always conscious of where we have been, savoring the satisfaction that we have lived life "holy and pleasing to God."

> *So live, that when thy summons comes to join*
> *The innumerable caravan, which moves*
> *To that mysterious realm, where each shall take*
> *His chamber in the silent halls of death,*
> *Thou go not, like the quarry-slave at night,*
> *Scourged to his dungeon, but, sustained and soothed*
> *By an unfaltering trust, approach thy grave,*
> *Like one that wraps the drapery of his couch*
> *About him, and lies down to pleasant dreams.*
> *—William Cullen Bryant*
> *"Thanatopsis"*

Five

Confident Choices

Deborah's incredible success as a female judge and military leader resulted from: **(a)** *the obvious lack of male leadership,* **(b)** *her direct pipeline to God as a prophetess,* **(c)** *her administrative capabilities and self-confidence,* **(d)** *her deeply held conviction that women are fully equal with men.*

A woman commander-in-chief? Unbelievable even today, let alone back in the patriarchal, militaristic society of Old Testament times. And why Deborah? It might be understandable if she were the only living heir in a royal bloodline, but there is no biblical evidence that that was the case. In fact, the Bible gives no genealogy for Judge Deborah. All we know about this remarkable woman leader is that she was married to a man named Lapidoth, who is mentioned only once. There is no hint of family or political connections. Her name suddenly appears in the biblical text, without explanation and as if her gender were not a factor.

In many respects Deborah is the most enviable career woman of the Old Testament. I have often thought that if I could change places with one Old Testament character it would be Deborah. Her daily routine involved going to the office, so to speak, under a palm tree that was named for her, located "between Ramah and Bethel in the hill country of Ephraim" (Judg. 4:5). No two days were alike, and there was no time for boredom to set in; her schedule was full and her activities varied, though much of her time was devoted to listening to problems and arbitrating disputes between

71

ordinary people. She was far more than a small-town judge, however. As the ruler of all Israel she made confident choices that affected the nation for generations to come.

Deborah was no caretaker executive, and she certainly was not a token woman. She was a courageous and forceful ruler who stood head and shoulders above most of the other judges who ruled Israel during this period, many of whom were only marginally qualified for the job. How she attained her position is not recorded, but it is evident that she enjoyed the confidence of the people as well as her top military aide, Barak. In fact, Barak refused to go into battle without her. And when she did accompany him, she did so not in her own strength, but confidently as a prophetess in close contact with the Almighty.

Despite the incredibly unfavorable odds—outnumbered ten to one—her army won the battle in "the first large-scale operation against a major foe of all Israel." Then, through expert diplomacy, she forged an alliance with the northern tribes which resulted in a unity that had not been accomplished under any prior ruler. The "battle was also pivotal in the salvation-history of the tribes," because never again would the armies of the Canaanites wage full-scale war on Israel.[1]

But Deborah was more than a great "warrior," as one author has hailed her, for her military success ushered in forty years of peace. Her reign as a diplomatic and peacemaking judge stands as a monument to responsible government.

What was her secret? How did she rise to such heights in a world where women were treated as slaves at worst and second-class citizens at best? How did she win the respect of those around her?

A detailed description of Deborah's style of leadership is not recorded, but the very fact that she marshaled an army of ten thousand men and led that force into battle tells us something about her extraordinary capacity to gain trust in demanding circumstances. Surely there must have been jealous petty officers or high-ranking military men who considered themselves better qualified than this female judge. Yet her authority prevailed, apparently without challenge—at least none is recorded. Something about her character must have exuded confidence and radiated self-assurance that was not threatening to the men around her. Perhaps because her inner confidence was not based on her own qualifications and strength but on the Lord's.

Assured of the Lord's guidance, Deborah made confident choices that brought Israel through a difficult time in history.

"O Lord," she sang in her song of praise and victory, "when you marched . . . the earth shook" (Judg. 5:4). She and her men were warriors, but the "righteous acts of the Lord" were equated with the "righteous acts of his warriors" (5:11). It was the Lord who brought the victory; it was the Lord who was doing the marching and giving the marching orders. The song ends with that same note of confidence in the Lord: "May they who love you be like the sun when it rises in its strength" (5:31).

Deborah and the other women who blazed trails through the uncharted wilderness of a man's world provide us with role models that bolster our confidence as we make choices that often parallel theirs. Indeed, it is sad that history and biography are often considered specialized subjects with little or no relevance to the ordinary individual. They do have relevance. And it is vital that we discover this heritage and become friends of those who have gone before. We ought to stand on their shoulders as we face the same obstacles that confronted them.

Though separated by time and geography, Deborah is one of us. No doubt she emerged from girlhood with the same insecurities we face. She was a woman in a culture that would not let her forget that fact. But God had a mission for her that would take her beyond gender limitations and force her to realize that the source of her strength rested in him alone.

So ought it to be with us. Our confidence in decision making must grow out of the inner certainty that we are operating on the strength of the Lord. Unfortunately we often find this difficult to identify and grasp. It is all too easy to derive our strength from our own capabilities; and when these fail us, our confidence plummets.

Making confident choices does not come naturally to most people, and this is particularly true for women. From early childhood our culture encourages us to rely on others for important decision making and protection. Many of us have been repeatedly reminded that man is the "head" of woman and that marriage demands a submissive spirit rather than self-sufficiency and confidence.

In every generation since Adam and Eve sinned in the Garden of Eden, women have struggled with the misuse of male headship. Susanna Wesley is an example of the way women have been denied the God-given responsibility of confident decision making and have suffered for it. Her husband, Samuel, did not even permit her to voice her own opinion in politics. When she refused to say "Amen" to his prayer for King William of Orange, whom she regarded as a usurper to the throne, Samuel abandoned her and their children with the remonstrance, "If we have two kings, we must have two beds."

Susanna's response is classic, placing the blame for their separation squarely on him: "Since I am willing to let him quietly enjoy his opinions, he ought not to deprive me of my little liberty of conscience." She recognized that as a whole person she could not be deprived of her own conscience and choices, and that without her "little liberty of conscience" she would essentially lose her personhood.

When the king died, Samuel returned home, but Susanna was never the same. She had developed an inner strength that served her well in making confident choices.[2]

What about headship and submission? Do these concepts restrict women and impede them from making confident choices? They certainly have that potential. If a woman is under the authority of a man and her primary response to that man is submission, then her real choices belong to that man.

The "tie-breaker illustration" is often used in characterizing the husband's role in marriage. When there are choices to be made, agreement between the husband and wife is ideal; but if that ideal is absent, the husband becomes the tie-breaker. For example, if the wife's choice is to return to college and finish her degree, but the husband's choice is that she stay home and devote her time to cleaning and meal preparation, then the husband's choice goes into operation.

The concepts of headship and submission are among the least understood in the whole of Scripture. The problem arises out of the common usage of the word *head* in English. The basic dictionary definition of *head* in both Greek and English is simply that part of the body that extends upward from the neck. On this meaning there is no debate. But in English a second major meaning of *head* is that of leader or ruler. We use the word this way when we speak of the head of a corporation or the head of a delegation. So when we encounter the word *head* (*kephale* in Greek) in the Bible, it is only natural to give it the English meaning of ruler, even though that meaning is not necessarily its primary meaning in the Greek.

The concept of headship—man as head of the woman— is said to be rooted in Creation. Yet look closely at the Creation account and you will find no reference to the man being the *ruler* of the woman. It is only as a result of the Fall and the Curse that Eve is told that her husband will rule over her (Gen. 3:16), and now through Christ's redemption we are beyond the Curse. How, then, is the man the head of woman in Creation? He is her *source* or *origin*, for the Bible tells us that woman was taken from man in Creation. This is further clarified in 1 Corinthians 11, where we read that the head of woman is man, but nowhere in this passage is there any reference to rulership. Headship can clearly be understood from the context to mean source or origin: "For as woman *came from* man, so also man is *born of* woman. But everything *comes from* God" (1 Cor. 11:12, italics mine).

This meaning of *head* allows us to view Deborah in proper perspective. Some writers have suggested that she "wore the pants" in the family and that Lapidoth may very well have been the proverbial henpecked husband. But the Bible gives no indication of this. Deborah is simply the one who fills the leadership role. She is properly defined as *ruler* but not as *source*, and there is no indication that her role was one that was deemed by God to be inappropriate for a woman.

Once the meaning of *head* is clarified, the issue of submission falls easily into place. Ephesians 5:21 admonishes us to "submit to one another out of reverence for Christ." This includes all Christians, women and men. Nor should submission be viewed negatively as an exercise in groveling. *Submit* is a verb that takes only the active form. As such, it is something we do of our own volition, with the assurance that it will not hinder us from making confident choices. In fact, the very opposite is true. Submission to God and to others ought to bolster our confidence in decision making.

For Deborah, making confident choices clearly involved submission. First and foremost, she submitted to God; thereafter she submitted to those under her. When Barak refused to go into battle alone, she submitted to his demand

and went with him; yet there is not a hint that she relinquished any of her authority.

Decision making is a skill, and the more we practice it, the more confident and proficient we become. Deborah became an experienced decision-maker as she daily arbitrated disputes under the palm tree. No doubt she drew on those same skills as she faced momentous decisions in battle.

Deborah is the exception to the rule, however. Most women in patriarchal societies are schooled in the art of submission and given little authority over any area of life. Oh, we make decisions all right—daily ones that keep our home and life running—but most of them seem rather inconsequential when pitted against the bigger "battles" of life. They are important in that they force us to draw strength from God and offer some experience in building confidence in decision making. However, deciding what to do about the minor choices in life will not automatically prepare us for the major ones. Our choices are interrelated, and if we confine ourselves—or let ourselves be confined— to the inconsequential, we neglect our God-given responsibilities and discard our decision-making capabilities by default.

The late Catherine Marshall unwittingly fell into this trap. When she was a young wife and mother, her husband Peter was the "head of the home"—the decision-maker. He made the important decisions and took care of all the business and financial matters. She did the housekeeping, cooked the meals, and cared for their young son. When her husband died suddenly, she was utterly unprepared to take charge. "In many ways, I was still a little girl," she writes. "I had never once figured out an income tax blank, had a car inspected, consulted a lawyer, or tried to read an insurance policy."[3]

Intelligent choices are based on knowledge and experience. If we fail to do our homework and adequately investigate matters, we have no basis for confident decision making. We cannot be confident in our choice of a college or in the purchase of a computer, for example, unless we have done the necessary "comparative shopping."

But what about those matters that require decisive action—the ones that do not offer the luxury of homework preparation? In these instances we must turn to premeditated choices—those "what if" situations we have intentionally thought through in order to anticipate the unexpected.

I'm a "what if" sort of person. There are very few potential situations or problems in life that I have not at one time or another thought through. I mentally work through conversations and arguments that may never arise, but in the process I'm honing my decision-making skills. Then when emergencies do arise and the adrenalin flows, I'm prepared with a variety of options.

But that is part of my nature. For many people, however, the opposite is true. They almost become paralyzed when they are forced to make choices, particularly in a crisis situation. And this problem is certainly not limited to the female gender. Men struggle with indecisiveness as much as women do. Norman Vincent Peale, known for his popular books on positive thinking, is an example. His wife, Ruth, writes about her own decision-making ability and her husband's utter inability to function in that area. "I never had any problem making up my mind about almost anything," she says, "but he had a hard time making decisions." On one occasion when he was unable to make a choice between two churches that were calling him as pastor and his vacillating finally got the best of Ruth, she gave an ultimatum: they would go into a closed room and stay there until he was able to make a decision. After an afternoon and evening of confinement, he finally came to his decision.[4]

Here again premeditation and planning could have

relieved the strain. Had Peale established priorities and goals and mulled over ahead of time what he would do should two churches call him at the same time—certainly not an unlikely circumstance for one in the ministry—the decision-making process might have gone much more smoothly from the beginning.

For some women the inability to make confident choices stems from low self-esteem. If a woman does not value herself, she will not value her choices. Unfortunately our self-worth tends to focus too largely on *self*. We subconsciously believe that somehow our worth depends on our physical beauty or our social standing or our intelligence or education.

Confident choices depend on a healthy self-image, and a healthy self-image is derived from nothing other than the acknowledged reality that we are created in the very *image* of God. I often think it is easier for men to accept this reality. From the time we are little children we learn to picture God as a male being, forgetting that Genesis 1:27 tells us that humanity—male and female—was created in the image of God. God is spirit, not a flesh-and-blood man; but God is also a person with an *image*, and both men and women reflect that image.

When I'm tempted to ask *Who am I?* or *Why am I here?* the answer emerges, as simple as it is profound, and gives me all the reassurance I need. *Who am I?* I am a woman. *Why am I here?* To reflect the image of God. Indeed, there I am in the first chapter of the Bible, created in the image of almighty God. And it is there I must discover my true self-image.

Once we have established this basis for a healthy self-image, we must then take our attention off ourselves and focus it on God and on others. In keeping with this, Eugenia Price offers the advice *Leave Yourself Alone* in both the title and the contents of one of her perceptive books, with the subtitle adding further caution, "Set Yourself Free from the Paralysis of Self-Analysis." Too much self-analysis does paralyze our ability to make confident choices that must have an outward, rather than inward, focus.

It is important to ask ourselves, *How much have we really gained in this "me generation"?* Bookstores, publishers, and authors have prospered on self-help books, while therapists have built entire practices on exploring and enhancing our self-images. But have we really gained confidence and become better women in the process?

When it comes to self, the problem most of us face is more likely one of self-centeredness and pride and an inflated sense of ourselves. David Meyers, a professor of psychology at Hope College in Holland, Michigan, makes this point. In *The Inflated Self* Meyers repudiates the supposedly almost universal problem of low self-esteem. He discovered that in reality people tend to think of themselves, as the Bible warns, "more highly than they ought" (Rom. 12:3). In other words, the average person thinks of himself or herself as above average. In another book he writes: "In virtually every area that is subjective and socially desirable, most people see themselves as better than average." He goes on to give specific examples:

> When the college board asked high school seniors to compare themselves with others their own ages, 60 percent reported themselves better than average in athletic ability, only 6 percent below average. In leadership ability, 70 percent rated themselves above average, 2 percent below average. In ability to get along with others, zero percent of the 829,000 students who responded rated themselves below average while 60 percent saw themselves in the top ten percent and 25 percent put themselves in the top 1 percent.[5]

Some specialists in low-self esteem insist that one of the telltale signs of a low self-image is magnifying one's own importance. This is no doubt true. But the above statistics are from a cross-section of the population, not the test scores of the underachieving bully down the street whose trademark is one-upmanship.

Such statistics and observations ought to be taken seriously. An inflated sense of self can lead to over-confidence, and we must never mistake over-confident choices for confident choices. The latter grow out of optimism rooted in our profound trust in God and from a realism that flows out of an objective assessment of ourselves. Over-confident choices, on the other hand, are often the product of self-aggrandizement, which leads to false hopes and failures.

Deborah was a woman of confident choices. A contemporary woman who fits that description is Roberta Hestenes, featured in a cover story of *Christianity Today* entitled "Taking Charge." Like Deborah, she stands out as a leader in a man's world. She is president of Eastern College in St. Davids, Pennsylvania, and is the first woman college president among the schools of the Evangelical College Coalition. But her role as a Christian leader was established long before she was called to this position, and not without controversy. On one occasion a supporter of World Vision vowed he would no longer contribute to the organization because Roberta—a woman—was a member of the board of directors. When told that she was a highly capable and dedicated worker, he responded, "I don't mind a woman doing the work. I just don't want one to have that position." But such opposition did not stifle her. Like Deborah, she has responded to the voice of God; which sometimes means she has to turn a deaf ear to the voice of man.

Roberta has been described as a "powerful" woman; not politically or militarily, as Deborah was, but powerful in her own spheres of Christian ministry. "As the activist chairman of World Vision," writes Tim Stafford, "she exerts power in one of the largest parachurch organizations in the world."

And, like Deborah, she did not acquire her position through a royal bloodline or family connections.

Roberta Louis was born to a sixteen-year-old mother and seventeen-year-old father who married and moved into a garage in order to provide this unwanted child with a family. It was a dysfunctional family at best, disfigured by alcoholism and anger. But from her earliest years, Roberta was a survivor. She excelled in school and entered California's Whittier College on a scholarship.

It was at college that she found faith in Christ, and her conversion was electric. "I read my Bible," she recalls, "and every word leaped off the page." Almost immediately she started a campus Bible study where dozens of students professed faith in Christ, though not without opposition from the college administration. Even her Lutheran church opposed her enthusiasm for evangelism. After sixteen of her sixth-grade Sunday school boys were converted, her pastor asked her to leave the church.

This early taste of success in evangelism inflamed Roberta's passion for full-time Christian work. "I wanted more than anything else to serve Christ," she says, "to win people to Christ, to teach people about Christ. The classical way you did that, as a Christian woman, was to find a Christian man who would commit to full-time Christian service, and to marry him." Following that traditional game plan, she married John Hestenes; but her dream of spending her life as a career missionary in Latin America did not materialize. John's interests gravitated more toward nuclear physics than evangelism and church planting.

Thinking her ministry was dependent upon her husband and realizing, therefore, that a career in missions was not an option was a blow to Roberta. "Something just died in me." But like Deborah, she began to discover that a married woman can have a ministry apart from her husband, even when her role is the more prominent one. John Hestenes remains in the background, and twice he has agreed to changes in location and in his own career in order to further his wife's ministry. At present, while Roberta carries out her "presidential" duties and wields power in the Christian community, John carries out his research in biophysics at Drexel University. He recognizes that God has uniquely gifted his wife, a fact that strengthens her confidence: "He will come to church especially to hear me preach because he says God blesses him through it."

Roberta is a woman of confident choices, evidenced by her pilgrimage to Christian ministry. She knew from the beginning that she was entering a man's world and that there would be obstacles along the way. While serving as director of adult education on a church staff, she sensed the powerlessness of women in ministry and was tempted to move into secular work. Her pastor pleaded with her to stay and dedicate her gifts to the church. "I heard that as a call from God," she recalls. "I went back to the church, not knowing that it was going to work out, but knowing that that's what my call was."

That call was pivotal, and it propelled her into a series of choices that led her to where she is today. But, like Deborah's, her confidence has been rooted in a sense of humility and dependence on God. For Roberta there is no room for bitterness or anger or defiance. "I have not been an angry woman pushing on doors that people wouldn't let me go through," she emphasizes. "I've been a reluctant woman, and people have said, 'Come and help.' And I have said, 'No, no, you can't possibly mean me.' They've said, 'Yes, we do,' and when I got there they meant it. My theme has to be gratitude. I love Christian work. The opportunity to teach the Bible, to lead people to Christ, to build a group program—I have always been very, very grateful for that."

It was as a professor at Fuller Theological Seminary that Roberta first began to make her mark on the larger

Christian world. After some years, however, she realized that her ideals for Christian seminary education were competing and conflicting with the ideals of others. When her vision for a curriculum centered on Christian formation and discipleship did not come to fruition, she began to look for another setting in which to develop her goals. That she found as president of Eastern College.[6]

Roberta Hestenes's story is an inspiring one, but it is tempting to think that it's an exception to the rule, and thus an example that is not relevant to most of us. She seems to have everything going for her. But when we analyze her life we see an individual who might have withered on the vine had she not early in life begun making confident choices.

Confident choices may seem unfeminine or out of character for many women, but we can all bring vigor and vitality to our decision making if we apply biblical principles and ask ourselves perceptive questions.

- On what am I basing my confidence? Am I focusing negatively on my weight or positively on my new clothes? Or am I drawing my confidence from God, recognizing that I as a woman am made in his image?
- Have I wrongly believed that the Bible teaches confident choices and leadership are for men only? Do I unconsciously assume that confident choices lead to power-grabbing rather than the servanthood ideal that Jesus emphasized?
- Do I like women of confident choices, or do I secretly resent them, thinking they are overstepping their bounds—or at least the bounds I am comfortable with? Do I have role models who are women of confident choices?
- Does decisive decision making come naturally to me, or do I need to work out premeditated choices to implement in case of emergencies?
- Have I avoided leadership because I have confused a

male style of leadership with leadership itself? Do I diminish my diplomatic and problem-solving skills, thinking they are not consistent with an effective leadership style?

Deborah's "victory hymn," recorded in Judges 5, gives the glory for the Israelites' victory in battle to Yahweh, the God of Israel. The Lord God is the main character; she is only a secondary figure. I believe that if Roberta—and others like her—had a victory hymn, it too would give all the glory to the Lord. She would be only a minor character in the pilgrimage that has carried her through her confident choices in life.

So do not throw away your confidence; it will be richly rewarded. You need to persevere so that when you have done the will of God, you will receive what he has promised.
—Hebrews 10:35–36

Six

Better Choices

Mary of Bethany made a better choice than her sister Martha because: (a) she focused her attention on Jesus, (b) meal preparation and housework do not have the eternal value that learning does, (c) she placed leisure above mundane household chores, (d) she challenged the cultural norms of her day.

Mary, Martha, and Lazarus. Were they two "old maids" and their bachelor brother living together? Scripture gives few details about the family dynamics. There are hints that Martha may have been the older of the two sisters and was probably the owner of the family home; yet Mary seems to have been the more prominent one in their community of Bethany, referred to as "the village of Mary and her sister Martha" (John 11:1). But in the biblical record they are given equal recognition, while at the same time shown to be unique women with very different character traits.

They had much in common, as sisters often do, and they functioned as one in time of crisis. When their brother Lazarus was gravely ill, they together sent word of the emergency to Jesus. But when he finally arrived—after Lazarus died—their responses seem to fit their individual personalities.

Martha, the woman of action, went to meet Jesus, expressing her bitter disappointment that he had not come sooner, but holding out the hope that he could still perform a miracle. Mary waited at the house and only went out to meet Jesus after he had asked for her. She also expressed disappointment at Jesus' failure to come sooner, but did so while weeping prostrate at his feet (John 11:1–32).

The scene that most sets these sisters apart, however, occurred when Jesus was invited to the home of the two sisters. At that time, Mary sat at Jesus' feet treasuring every word he spoke, while Martha set about preparing a meal. Yet when she ventured to ask for Mary's help, pointing out her thoughtlessness, Martha was rebuked by the very one she was seeking to please. "Mary has chosen what is better," Jesus said (Luke 10:42).

In countless Bible studies and discussions women have wondered aloud whether Jesus was really being fair in this situation, especially considering the circumstances. This was more than just another instance of sibling rivalry. Martha had a legitimate gripe. Food preparation in first-century Palestine was a complicated ordeal—without refrigerators, microwave ovens, and blenders.

I am reminded of this whenever I am entertained by my Kenyan friends who cook on an outdoor wood fire. I marvel at the skill and efficiency of my hostess, who may have a mother-in-law or child assisting, but never allows her guests to hang around the "kitchen" helping with last-minute preparations. Guests are special, and as such they are kept apart, talking together in separate quarters, perhaps similar to the setup in Martha's home in Bethany.

It is not difficult, then, to understand Martha's irritation. She was busy, and she needed the help that only a member of the household could give. Martha had every reason to be annoyed with her sister. Still, that was not the issue. The lesson here is not that Martha's work should be devalued, but that our activities have differing values and priorities. Mary knew that her times with Jesus were limited and that, therefore, meal preparation was secondary. So Mary made the *better* choice.

Most women could at one time or another put themselves into either woman's shoes. I would like to think that at least sometimes I'm a Mary, focusing on those things with the greater value. Certainly the dust on my furniture would seem to serve as evidence for this mentality. When the choice is between dusting or playing Ping-Pong with my son, it's no contest. Soon he will be away at college, but the dust will still be there to dust, if I feel so inclined.

At times, though, I'm a Martha, too busy to savor the moment. Consumed by mundane details, I lose sight of what really matters. That's when I need to be reminded to choose what is better and make my time with the Lord and with family and friends a top priority.

Unfortunately some choices are not so easy or clear-cut. We must remember that Jesus did not tell Martha that she made the *wrong* choice—only that Mary chose what was *better*. Sometimes it is difficult to determine what is good, what is better, and what is best. Yet the story of Mary and Martha does offer a time-worn principle that fits many of the situations that confront us: Life is short, so choose that which counts for eternity.

This principle was demonstrated another time by Mary, when once again Jesus affirmed her choice. In this instance she had anointed him with very expensive perfume (John 12:1–8). When the disciple Judas objected, pointing out that Mary was wasting perfume worth a year's wages which could have been more wisely used to help the poor, Jesus rebuked him. In doing so, Jesus was certainly not ignoring those living in poverty. He had previously told a rich official who came to him for spiritual counsel that to inherit eternal life he must sell all he had and give it to the poor. Mary, however, did not need to prove her commitment to Jesus in that manner. In her case, selling the perfume and using the money to assist those in need would have been a *good* choice, but anointing her Savior was a *better* choice.

Choosing what is better, as Mary did, is aided by long-range planning and established standards that can be quickly accessed for everyday choices. These are the kinds of decisions we have anticipated far in advance; consequently we have had time to weigh the merits of the various options. But most of our choices come upon us with little warning. And for these we need practical principles that can be put into operation at a moment's notice, turning decision making into a smooth and natural process.

One foundational principle is that a schedule—a set routine—is not a sacred icon. In our schedule-driven society it is natural to regard interruptions as unfortunate predicaments. We quickly learn how to avoid them or escape them, not recognizing that interruptions are often what make life most meaningful. "The great thing, if one can," wrote C. S. Lewis, "is to stop regarding all the unpleasant things as interruptions of one's 'own,' or 'real' life. The truth is of course that what one calls the interruptions are precisely one's real life—the life God is sending one day by day."[1]

My African friends have taught me to appreciate interruptions. If you arrive unexpectedly at their home you will never hear the words, "Is there something you need?" or "Can I help you with something?"—implying that you would not interrupt them unless you were facing some dire situation. Instead, they welcome you like a long-lost relative, insisting that, at the very least, you come in and share a cup of *chai*. If you do have a problem you need to discuss or a private matter to share, it can come out naturally in the conversation; you are not required to declare the purpose of your visit at the door.

Choosing what is better often means choosing to accept interruptions in our routine. That's what Martha should have done. Nor should she have been surprised when Jesus rebuked her for not doing so. He was a close friend, and she had many opportunities to observe his own response in such situations. Indeed, Jesus repeatedly heeded the interruptions in his daily activities rather than following the set course his disciples thought proper. When Bartimaeus shouted out for Jesus to have mercy on him, Jesus stifled the rebukes of his disciples by demonstrating compassionate concern (Mark 10:46–52). In choosing to allow the interruption, he chose what was better.

Besides demonstrating it, Jesus repeatedly taught this principle. Sometimes he used hyperbole: To the disciple who wanted to bury his father before following Jesus, the Master responded, "Follow me, and let the dead bury their own dead" (Matt. 8:22). Burying a parent was surely as worthy an activity as the meal preparation that consumed Martha, but Jesus' challenge to both was, *Choose what is better*. To his disciples who were vying for power, Jesus admonished, "If anyone wants to be first, he must be the very last, and the servant of all" (Mark 9:35). Here again, choosing what is better is the reverse of the world's values.

Sometimes the choice is not between what is good and what is better, but between what is bad and what is worse. Here we fall into what is often termed "situational ethics," a concept utterly abhorrent to absolutists. There is no gray area in ethical and moral issues, they argue, and we cannot make ethical and moral choices based on a particular situation.

A more responsible version of situational ethics has come to be known as "hierarchical ethics," which affirms absolutes, but not necessarily in all situations. For example, lying: lying is wrong, hierarchical ethicists would maintain; but lying may be the right thing to do if you can deter a rapist by telling him your estranged husband has tested positive for AIDS. In this instance the choice is between what is bad and what is worse.

Those who argue for hierarchical ethics point to Jesus as a model, citing such instances as his defense of breaking the sabbath. He made an Old Testament analogy: "Have you never read what David did when he and his companions were hungry and in need? In the days of Abiathar the high priest, he entered the house of God and ate the consecrated bread, which is lawful only for priests to eat. And he also gave some to his companions" (Mark 2:25–26).

This was not a principle Jesus used on a regular basis, nor should we. Most situations allow us to choose what is better rather than what is simply good. But when the only choice before us is the lesser of two evils, we must be prepared to make it—and be prepared to face possibly painful and devastating consequences. This might mean that a child disregards the biblical command to "honor one's father" when he or she reports him to the authorities in order to put a stop to sexual abuse. When a battered woman separates from her husband, thus breaking her wedding vows, she makes this same kind of choice.

Sometimes our sincere attempt to choose what is better pulls us in conflicting directions. The decision process is often agonizing, and we are left wondering if we have really made the right choice. This was true with Dorie Van Stone and her family.

Dorie and her husband Lloyd were convinced that God had called them to be missionaries to Irian Jaya, a region of the world that was largely unreached by the gospel. They left their loved ones and physical comforts behind to bring the message of Jesus to the "stone-age" Dani tribe deep in the Baliem Valley. Yet they carried with them a sense of security, knowing they were supported by the prayers and finances of friends and churches back home and by the counsel and guidance of their mission family and support team. The work was difficult but fruitful, and the Van Stones were convinced they were where God wanted them to be—until they were suddenly faced with a crisis that forced them to make the most difficult decision of their lives.

The year was 1959, and the Van Stones were settling into their second term of ministry with the Danis. During the first term Dorie had taught their children at home, but the standard policy of their mission board was that missionary children be educated in boarding schools. So when the Van Stones returned for their second term on the field, Darlene and Burney were sent away to school. Darlene, age eight, adjusted to the change; Burney, age nine, did not. For him, the thought of leaving his parents was unbearable. But mission policy prevailed, and Dorie and Lloyd, by their own testimony, "forced him to stay at the school."

"As we saw it, we had no alternative," recalls Dorie. "In accepting the missionary call, we had realized we would have to sacrifice. We also believed we must be totally obedient to the mission society. That meant Burney and Darlene *had* to go to school . . . away from their home, or we would have to return to the United States."

As wrenching as the separation was, Dorie accepted the agony as part of the cross she had to bear—until that day in 1959 when a message came that Burney had run away. The staff and students had searched in vain. Burney was nowhere to be found. Dorie's heart sank. "Something within us died," she remembers. Later that same day Burney was found hiding in a small aircraft, comforted by his childish hopes that he would be returned home undiscovered.

A one-week leave to visit his family did not relieve Burney's anxieties, and the next separation was more traumatic than ever. Burney clung to Dorie. She had to forcibly pry him away. How could she do it? Her only justification was that "God had called us to the Baliem Valley." It was not just a feeling, but an "unmistakable, direct, clear" call. Dorie and Lloyd prayed more fervently than ever that Burney would adjust, but their prayers were not answered. "He would not eat, he did no schoolwork, and he even refused to speak," writes Dorie. "When I arrived [at the school] he had been sobbing for two days."

Before her was the choice she had been dreading. "I wanted with all my heart to win the Danis. But my first responsibility was to win Burney and Darlene. . . . Unresolved conflicts churned within us. God had called us, yet now we had to return."

The Van Stones returned to the States, but the scars remained. Their doubts and the pain continued, at times exacerbated by others, such as the woman in a church they were visiting who challenged Dorie, "Why didn't you trust God? He'd have taken care of you and your children." No doubt Dorie's response was not what the woman anticipated. She broke down and wept.

The fact is that Dorie *was* trusting God. But despite that trust God had allowed her to be torn in two by the most difficult choice of her life. Her daughter, Darlene, summed up the circumstances in a profound but simple question: "Why does Jesus ask us to do such hard things?"[2]

As difficult as it often is to know which is the *better* choice when we are pulled in two directions, it is important to realize that the Bible does offer some specific examples of what types of choices are truly better. One of these examples is remarkably fitting for the circumstances that plagued the Van Stones who were struggling between their commitment to sacrifice their lives to the Lord and obedience to his voice regarding their family life. Samuel counseled Saul: "Does the Lord delight in burnt offerings and sacrifices as much as in obeying the voice of the Lord? To obey is better than sacrifice" (1 Sam. 15:22).

The book of Proverbs also offers a number of "better thans" to serve as guides in our decision making.

Proverbs 16:16 admonishes: "How much better to get wisdom than gold, to choose understanding rather than silver!" Many of our choices could be simplified by using that principle alone. Wealth is not bad, but wisdom is better.

Proverbs 16:19 offers a different slant on the same issue: "Better to be lowly in spirit and among the oppressed than to share plunder with the proud." Here the issue is not wealth versus wisdom, but being oppressed as opposed to being the oppressor. Most of us do not envision ourselves as oppressors; yet we are just that when because of our actions another feels oppressed. We all have been oppressors at one time or another, and we all have experienced oppression. When the choice is ours, the Scripture clearly tells us which is better. Another version of this same proverb is that it is better to be honest and poor than to be dishonest and rich.

Proverbs 21:9, which is repeated in Proverbs 25:24, has never been one of my favorite proverbs: "Better to live on a corner of the roof than share a house with a quarrelsome wife." Nor has Proverbs 21:19: "Better to live in a desert than with a quarrelsome and ill-tempered wife." But if we make these "better thans" gender neutral, there is a powerful message relating to living arrangements in general. It is better to get out of the way—to live on a roof, so to speak—than to remain in the presence of one who is being argumentative or ill-tempered. How many serious problems within families and among roommates could be avoided if this choice were made more wisely.

"Better" choices are ones that force us to evaluate our priorities. They are not ones that necessarily present clear-cut absolutes of right and wrong, but ones that demand we stop and take inventory of our lives. In doing this, I have found it helpful to formulate some "better than" proverbs. It might be profitable for all of us to adapt this little exercise to our own circumstances.

- Better to enjoy the love and admiration of a child than to win the applause and praise of a lecture hall assembly.

- Better to offer caring hospitality than a clean house when company arrives.
- Better to spend the hour wait in a doctor's office reading than to spend it explaining to the receptionist that my time is valuable too.
- Better to invest time in true friends than in those who are trading favors to climb the ladder of success.
- Better to accept criticism and learn from it than to be defensive and oversensitive.
- Better to focus on lifestyle and relationships than on offers of promotions and prestige.
- Better to enjoy summer fun on the shoreline of a lake than to buy a used boat with no warranty. (There's a story behind that one!)
- Better to be generous with my money than to save it all for retirement.

Choosing what is better ought to be a pattern for all our choices, not just those relating to big-ticket items such as where to go to college, what career/ministry to pursue, who to marry, how many children to have, or where to retire. No matter how insignificant they may seem, our better choices are important: Do I turn on a soap opera or read a chapter of a book when I have an extra hour to myself? Do I walk across the street to give some encouragement to my neighbor, retired and living alone, when I see her clipping the bushes, or do I go back to my computer and hammer out a few more sentences? Choosing between a book and a soap opera is not a problem for me; for someone else it might be. The second choice is where I might run into difficulty. I would be tempted to convince myself that I ought not "waste" the time, when I know deep down in my heart that choosing what is better often means investing time in others.

On the other hand, for those who are prone to fritter away too much time talking over the back fence, the better choice in the second instance might very well be to get back to the computer. The same principle might have applied to Mary. Had she habitually neglected helping her sister in meal preparation in order to get in on the conversation among their visitors, Jesus' response might have been entirely different, considering the extra burden that would have fallen on Martha's shoulders.

Today, however, our lifestyles are different, so we can often accommodate both. I'm like Mary. I don't want to miss good conversation, so I do most of my meal preparation ahead of time or involve my guest in the preparation. Either way I'm not left out.

The story of Mary and Martha ought not prompt us to take sides, with some supporting Martha by questioning the unfairness of her solitary kitchen patrol, and others supporting Mary by magnifying her spiritual perceptiveness.

Nor ought we imagine that *better* choices are the most desirable—as was the case with Mary and Martha. Probably most of us would much rather be in Mary's shoes, enjoying the conversation of guests, than slaving in a hot kitchen as Martha was doing.

Indeed, very often *better* choices are what appear to be the least desirable. When we would rather be walking in a peaceful, sunny field of flowers, God's *better* choice might be the dark, noisy, crime-ridden streets of an inner city. The decision is between what is good and what is better—in the eyes of God.

> *I said—"Let me walk in the fields,"*
> *He said—"No, walk in the town."*
> *I said—"There are no flowers there."*
> *He said—"No flowers, but a crown."*
> *I said—"But the skies are dark,*
> *There is nothing but noise and din."*
> *And He wept as He sent me back—*
> *"There is more," He said: "there is sin."*

I said—"I shall miss the light
  And friends will miss me, they say."
He answered—"Choose tonight
  If I am to miss you, or they."
I pleaded for time to be given,
  He said—"Is it hard to decide?
It will not be hard in Heaven
  To have followed the steps of your guide."

Then into His hand went mind,
  And into my heart came He,
And I walk in a light Divine,
  The path I had feared to see.
                    —George MacDonald (1824–1905)

Seven

Liberating Choices

The woman at the well made a liberating choice because: **(a)** *she was a liberated woman,* **(b)** *Jesus treated her with courtesy and respect,* **(c)** *she was sick of her old life that enslaved her,* **(d)** *Jesus made her an offer that she couldn't turn down.*

I recently heard a missionary speaker cynically describe the woman of Sychar as "a Samaritan chick who came sashaying up to Jesus" as he was sitting at the well. Somehow I don't think that's the way it happened. I think this man may have been reading his own fantasies into the text. To imagine the Samaritan woman as a flirtatious tease in sexy attire assumes far more than the story suggests. Fetching water was hard work, and the women usually drew water late in the day to avoid the worst of the heat. It was highly unlikely, then, that this woman expected to encounter anyone at the well at high noon, let alone a single male.

Most preachers and Bible commentators have difficulty understanding the woman at the well, perhaps because she was a woman—and a woman of ill repute at that. In the mind of John Calvin she was such a "forward and disobedient wife that she constrained her husbands to divorce her. . . . She did not cease to sin and prostituted herself to fornication." Once again these assumptions go far beyond the text.

We know nothing about the woman's previous five husbands or her relationships with them. Even to say that she was divorced five times is speculation. Indeed, it is

99

possible that she had been widowed five times. But whatever her situation in the past, Jesus focused on her present living arrangement. "The man you now have," he reminded her, "is not your husband" (John 4:18).

Who was this obscure woman who so providentially appeared at Jacob's well for this once-in-a-lifetime meeting with the living Messiah? Who was this paradox who suddenly rises out of the biblical text, never to be heard from again, yet functions as one of the most amazing evangelists in Scripture? "Many of the Samaritans from that town believed in him because of the woman's testimony, 'He told me everything I ever did'" (John 4:39). For this reason alone she is a woman we ought to take seriously as someone who offers us lessons from ancient Palestine for modern-day choices.

Who was she, this unnamed woman of Samaria? I close my eyes and try to picture her, but she eludes me. I cannot identify with her seeming carelessness for her reputation, and had I been her neighbor in Sychar, I probably would have avoided her. On the other hand, I may well have been drawn to that aspect of her personality that made her such a thinker—always doubting, always questioning.

When we try to grasp the essence of this woman, however, we really need to focus more on who she became after her incredible encounter with Jesus than on who she was previously. The before and after snapshots of her character and countenance bear little resemblance to each other. She had been "made over" by Jesus. As a result, she stands out as one of the first truly liberated women in all of history—liberated in every sense of the word.

Jesus began liberating the woman at the well the very moment he spoke to her as an equal. He did not treat her as though she were beneath him or as someone who needed to be pulled out of the sewer and saved. Instead, he treated her as one with whom he could dialogue on an equal level.

Their conversation, found in John 4:7–26, is one of the most fervent conversations ever recorded between Jesus and a woman. Indeed, when we compare the interaction Jesus had with this woman at Sychar to the interaction he had with the educated and prominent Nicodemus, the contrast is remarkable. John devotes as much space to this exchange as he does to the conversation with Nicodemus recorded in the previous chapter, which includes the oft-quoted John 3:16. The dialogue with the woman, however, involves twice as much interaction as does the dialogue with Nicodemus. At six points, John records, "the woman said to him" (or, "answered him"). Nicodemus, on the other hand, enters the conversation with Jesus only three times, and even then his questions seem less penetrating than the woman's.

Nicodemus asks Jesus if a person can return to the womb and be born again—his only specific inquiry. We must be careful not to judge Nicodemus too harshly, but in some ways this seems less than a brilliant question. Why didn't he ask if Jesus was alluding to some form of reincarnation and force the Messiah into a more in-depth discussion of the new birth?

The woman, on the other hand, asked weighty questions, inquiring about Jesus' status in comparison to the patriarch Jacob, about the geography of worship, and if the Messiah would be all-knowing. Her questions were not only personal but spiritually perceptive, and Jesus appears eager to dialogue and gives no indication that he finds her straightforward manner inappropriate. In fact, Jesus treats her with as much or more respect than he did the educated Pharisee. Nothing in this encounter suggests that she was an ignorant woman. Yet Abraham Kuyper, the well-known Dutch Reformed theologian and Bible teacher, found her contemptible, characterizing her as "positively uncouth," "superficial, mundane, and gullible."[1]

When I read his critical description of her, I almost wonder if we are analyzing the same biblical text. There is nothing in this passage that fits his description—least of all that she was gullible. Indeed, she was initially skeptical. Jesus told her outright that he was the Messiah. But when she returned to town to share the news, she framed her comment regarding his identity not as a dogmatic statement, but as a question: "Come, see a man who told me everything I ever did. Could this be the Christ?" (John 4:29).

The enthusiasm of her testimony indicates that she herself believed, but she was willing to let her neighbors make up their own minds. She no doubt realized that her reputation could hardly be an asset in her first witnessing venture, except that it offered her a new start and a chance to make that start public in the community.

She must have been all too conscious that the townspeople talked about everything she did, but always in whispers behind her back. In Jesus, however, she found someone who told her everything she ever did, lovingly and to her face. Thereafter, she, a woman and a despised Samaritan, was free not only to interact equally with a male Jew but also with the people of Sychar, proclaiming to them that the Messiah had come. She chose to move beyond the limitations of her past life, and she recognized that this could be done only by accepting the living water Jesus had to offer. In making this liberating choice she risked exposing herself to public scrutiny as she never had before, and in the process her life was transformed.

Jesus is the only one who can free us from the chains of our past—from the humiliation and sins that haunt us. And he is the only one who can free us from the chains of the present—from the barriers and obstacles that no amount of women's liberation can break down. We can never be fully liberated or make the right kinds of choices until we have encountered him, not just as Savior and Lord, but as a personal friend who fully understands all we are as women. We can trust him for this kind of friendship, as Dorothy Sayers expressed so well in these classic lines:

> Perhaps it is no wonder that the women were first at the Cradle and last at the Cross. They had never known a man like this Man. . . . A prophet and teacher who never nagged at them, never flattered or coaxed or patronized; who never made arch jokes about them, never treated them either as "The women, God help us!" or "The ladies, God bless them!"; who rebuked without querulousness and praised without condescension; who took their questions and arguments seriously; who never mapped out their sphere for them, never urged them to be feminine or jeered at them for being female; who had no axe to grind and no uneasy male dignity to defend; who took them as he found them and was completely unself-conscious.[2]

In recent decades there has been much talk of liberation. *Liberation theology* is widely viewed as the antidote for the problems of the world's oppressed. *Women's liberation* is seen as the cure-all for women's second-class status. And there are even some pockets of male discontent that champion *men's liberation.* These advocacy groups represent legitimate concerns, but when all is said and done, they offer little real freedom.

The Bible speaks directly to this issue. The apostle John, who records the story of the woman at the well and the freedom she found in Christ, goes on to talk about true liberation: "If you hold to my teaching, you are really my disciples. Then you will know the truth, and the truth will set you free . . . . Now a slave has no permanent place in the family, but a son belongs to it forever. So if the Son sets you free, you will be free indeed" (John 8:31–32, 35–36).

There is an interesting contrast in these verses: first we learn that the *truth* sets us free, and then we learn that without this truth we are essentially slaves. What, then, is true liberation? It is liberation from the slavery of false teaching.

The woman of Sychar made a liberating choice when she recognized that Jesus was the Messiah and that her own religious beliefs did not lead to that truth. But she was also set free from her enslavement by Jesus' recognition of her. It was a two-way acceptance: her acceptance of Jesus as the Christ, and his acceptance of her as a woman who was fully human and who needed no excuses for her gender.

The theme of liberation is not limited to Jesus' message. The entire Bible speaks to this issue—long before the advent of the modern women's liberation movement. Isaiah went so far as to suggest that liberated choices were a God-honoring substitute for fasting: "Is not this the kind of fasting I have chosen: to loose the chains of injustice and untie the cords of the yoke, to set the oppressed free and break every yoke" (Isa. 58:6). Women who feel enchained by their circumstances in a society that often fails to recognize their oppression can take courage from this passage.

Paul makes liberation a major theme of his letter to the Galatians, who were struggling with bondage to the law: "It is for freedom that Christ has set us free. Stand firm, then, and do not let yourselves be burdened again by a yoke of slavery" (Gal. 5:1). Anyone who trusts in Christ is set free, but that liberation is even more striking for those who have traditionally been on the outside.

In Old Testament times the rite of circumcision served as a sign of the covenant between God and his people. But no longer. "For in Christ Jesus neither circumcision nor uncircumcision has any value. The only thing that counts is faith . . ." (Gal. 5:6). The new sign that replaced circumcision was baptism—available to men and women alike. Women were now liberated and on an equal level with men, as Paul so powerfully declared: "There is no longer Jew or

Greek, there is no longer slave or free, there is no longer male and female, for all of you are one in Christ Jesus" (Gal. 3:28 NRSV).

We can claim this freedom as part of our inheritance in Christ, but even as we do we are confronted with a paradox. At the very moment we are liberated, we become enslaved again. "Live as free" people, Peter writes, but in that very same sentence he adds, "live as *servants* of God" (1 Peter 2:16, italics mine). Christ breaks our chains of slavery to sin only to transform us into his servants—liberated to serve.

Nowhere is this truth more powerfully illustrated than in the Christian pilgrimage of Kana, a woman from the Dani tribe of Irian Jaya.

"When the gospel came to us Dani people, we were told that the gospel was for the men," she recalls. "The men said we women did not have souls, so we did not need the gospel message. The men crowded around the speakers of the good news. We women were told to sit out on the edges of the crowd and keep the children quiet so the men could get all of the profit from the message."

So persuaded was Kana that she was not fully human and did not have a soul that she questioned her own existence.

"Once I was in a group when a photo was taken by the missionary. I was so excited I could not wait until the picture had been developed and came back. When word came that the picture had arrived, I elbowed my way through the crowd to see if my face would show up or if, as the men insisted, I would not appear because I was only a spirit." She was ecstatic when she recognized herself in the photo. "There I was! . . . I had shown up the same as the men had! I, too, was a real person!"

Kana realized for the first time that she was not only a real person but that she was liberated from the chains of male superiority that had enslaved her. But she soon recognized that the freedom she had so gloriously found in

Christ led her right back into another form of slavery. At the final message at a women's retreat she was confronted by the challenge of the Great Commission, and for the first time she came to grips with the responsibility that comes with freedom. It was a solemn moment.

"I lingered behind," she recalls. "I was battling with the Lord over this new thought that I was also responsible to carry the gospel to my unsaved neighbors." Kana soon found her hesitation combatted when other women perceived her inner conflict and vowed to gather her firewood and dig her gardens if she would reach out as an evangelist. Like the woman at the well, she made a liberated choice only to find herself a servant of Christ.[3]

True liberation, then, does result in servanthood. But as women we must be cautious that we do not exaggerate the significance of this enslavement or servanthood. While it is true that in one sense we are bond slaves to Christ, the term is a metaphor that emphasizes our subservience to Christ who is figuratively our master. It is in reality a volitional covenant relationship—a reciprocal arrangement. As we submit to Christ and serve him, we realize our own freedom.

But is this freedom anything more than pie-in-the-sky double-talk? Is it real? Karl Marx was convinced it was not. Religion, and particularly any concept of enslavement to Christ, was to him the odious "opiate of the people." In other words, Marx said, faith in God is a narcotic, a drug that so numbs rational thinking that it makes people satisfied with their lot when they should be bringing about change through revolution.

This is an issue that I have pondered over the years. Largely due to geographical considerations, I took doctoral studies at Northern Illinois University, one of the most Marxist graduate history departments in the country—at least according to an article in the *Wall Street Journal.* Small wonder, then, that as a result of my studies there I no longer take capitalism for granted and am more conscious of issues relating to class struggle. But I have also come to recognize the utter hopelessness of a philosophy of change that does not include faith in God. Marx's own family life illustrates this. His daughters, Eleanor and Laura, both committed suicide in an effort to end what they considered to be a meaningless existence. Marxism was not enough to meet their needs as whole persons.

So, too, women's liberation. If our liberating choices are based on a philosophy of feminism that is devoid of the Christian principles of servanthood and freedom in Christ, we may end up just as empty and disillusioned as Eleanor and Laura.

But before we dismiss Karl Marx's critique of religion entirely, we ought to at least concede that any religion that serves only as a drug to numb our senses is not true Christianity. Our faith in Christ ought to stir us to action and to raise our consciousness on issues of injustice and oppression. As such, our faith ought to be broad enough to assimilate that which is good and just in feminism (or Marxism, for that matter), and it ought to serve as well as we make liberated choices.

Feminism, despite its bad name in many Christian circles, has given women an array of liberated choices we might not have otherwise. Feminists were the radicals of the nineteenth century who demanded the privilege of higher education for women. Feminists of the early twentieth century fought for women's suffrage, and the freedom to use birth control. No longer must women give birth to eight or ten or more children. We have choices not readily available to our mothers and grandmothers.

Liberated choices in themselves, however, have no merit. *Liberated for what?* is the issue. Here is where we must take personal inventory. Are we truly liberated women, and where is that liberation taking us?

- Do I revel in the freedom spoken of by Jesus and Paul, while at the same time recognizing the responsibility it entails?
- Am I willing to risk making liberating choices and boldly reverse my direction if necessary?
- Am I using liberation for retaliation or self-indulgence and excess? Do I harbor feelings of bitterness and resent men?
- Are my liberated choices aligned with biblical—not the world's—liberation? Do they contribute to healthy growth in my relationship with God and with others?
- Do my liberated choices contribute to a healthy self-image—an image that is rooted in the image of God? Does it contribute to my self-development in a positive way?
- Is my liberated spirit contagious? Am I helping to free other women from unnecessary bondage?

Liberated choices are not always easy ones to make, and it's easy to become confused by what the world touts as liberation. When a liberated choice involves ending an abusive relationship, it can be viewed as healthy; but when it involves ending a marriage simply to explore new avenues and other relationships, it is liberation gone awry.

One of the best examples we have of a Christian woman modeling liberated choices comes from the African-American community and the late Ethel Waters, who grew up facing oppression from every direction. She was poor and black and female, and life offered her little hope, much less the freedom to make liberated choices.

Ethel was born on October 31, 1896, in a dilapidated tenement house in Philadelphia, Pennsylvania. Her mother was a twelve-year-old girl who had been raped at knife point. Little wonder that she grew up feeling rejected.

"I never belonged," she later recalled. "I never got the affection I so desperately wanted." When she was twelve, however, her life changed as profoundly as her mother's had at that young age—but Ethel's changed for the better. She attended a week-long Methodist revival meeting, where she made the first truly liberated choice of her life. Though she initially was convinced that even God could not accept a girl as unworthy as she, by the end of the week she was able to accept God's acceptance of her as her first step in her pilgrimage of faith.

Living the Christian life was not easy for Ethel as a young, black, inner-city girl still plagued by low self-esteem. Then the year after her conversion, at thirteen, she married a man ten years her senior. Her hope of finding acceptance in human form, however, faded as quickly as the marriage ended. Life went on, and Ethel struggled to make a living as a cleaning woman.

Her first real break came when she was invited to sing at a Philadelphia night club. The years that followed brought one achievement after another. By the 1940s she had become a celebrity. She made a movie with Warner Brothers, sang with Irving Berlin on Broadway, and became the first black woman to appear in a Broadway drama. She had more than fulfilled her wildest dreams, and more opportunities beckoned. She had made liberated choices that had in many ways eradicated the racism and sexism and poverty that had once oppressed her, but she still was not free. She longed for acceptance.

Then she finally found it—in 1957 when she dedicated her life to God at a Billy Graham Crusade in Madison Square Garden. Like the woman at the well, she was offered living water that became "a spring of water welling up to eternal life," and she was finally set free to soar—to rise above the bondage of this world.[4]

"They will soar on wings like eagles," writes the prophet Isaiah; "they will run and not grow weary, they will walk and not be faint" (Isa. 40:31). Those words reflected Ethel Waters's ensuing years of ministry with the Billy Graham Association. And yet, like all of us, there were many times when she had to reckon with her own limitations and weaknesses and listen for the words of Jesus, "Come to me, all you who are weary and burdened, and I will give you rest" (Matt.11:28).

Ethel Waters is probably best known for her powerful and poignant rendition of "His Eye Is on the Sparrow." Oh, how her voice would ring out with conviction as she sang the first lines of that chorus: "I sing because I'm happy; I sing because I'm *free*." Because she *was* free.

Like the woman at the well, she made liberated choices, and she, too, found true liberty in Christ.

> *Like the woman at the well, I was seeking*
> *   For things that could not satisfy,*
> *And then I heard my Savior speaking,*
> *   "Draw from My well that never shall run dry."*
>
> *There are millions in this world who are craving*
> *   The pleasures earthly things afford,*
> *But none can match the wondrous treasure*
> *   That I find in Jesus Christ my Lord.*
>
> *Fill my cup, Lord, I lift it up, Lord,*
> *   Come and quench this thirsting of my soul;*
> *Bread of Heaven, feed me till I want no more;*
> *   Fill my cup, fill it up and make me whole.*
> *   —Richard Blanchard*
> *   "Fill My Cup, Lord"*

Eight

Foolish Choices

Abigail's story is one of: **(a)** *codependency that needed a good dose of therapy,* **(b)** *a faithful wife who "stands by her man,"* **(c)** *a survivor who outlasted her debased husband,* **(d)** *a smart woman who made foolish choices.*

If Abigail were living today she might be considered a perfect candidate for a recovery group, perhaps Al-Anon or a support group for "women who love too much." Her profile also fits well with the women discussed in the best-selling book of a few years ago, *Smart Women, Foolish Choices.*

Abigail's story is found in 1 Samuel 25, sandwiched between two separate incidents when David spared King Saul's life. The writer of this book of Israel's history introduces us to Abigail with the poignant description: "She was an intelligent and beautiful woman, but her husband, a Calebite, was surly and mean in his dealings." A little later in the chapter her husband Nabal is described by his own servants as "such a wicked man that no one can talk to him," and further along we find him thoroughly intoxicated (1 Sam. 25:3, 17, 36).

Nabal was very wealthy, the owner of three thousand sheep and one thousand goats, but his wealth seemed little consolation to Abigail. To suggest that this was no fairy-tale marriage is an understatement, and it is hard to imagine how this woman endured all her husband's unpleasantness. She did seem, however, to be a fairly adept at covering for his inappropriate behavior. Indeed, her first recorded action is her effort to undo her husband's rebuff of David and his men.

David and his guerilla army of about six hundred men had been roving the desert near Carmel, where Nabal lived. From the biblical account it would seem that there were two basic options when it came to feeding and supplying this type of military force: simply taking what was necessary from local landowners like Nabal, or asking for it as payment for protecting the landowner's property. David chose the latter. He sent his men to Nabal, requesting the necessary provisions. The man's contemptuous rebuff, however, quickly prompted David to set in motion plans for the other option. "Put on your swords!" he ordered his men, and he and four hundred of his soldiers headed out to pay another visit to Nabal (25:13).

In the meantime, one of Abigail's servants who had overheard Nabal's insulting remarks to David's men reported the verbal exchange to Abigail and warned her of the impending disaster: "Abigail lost no time. She took two hundred loaves of bread, two skins of wine, five dressed sheep, five seahs of roasted grain, a hundred cakes of raisins and two hundred cakes of pressed figs, and loaded them on donkeys. Then she told her servants, 'Go on ahead; I'll follow you.' But she did not tell her husband Nabal" (25:18–19).

By the time Abigail reached David he had worked himself into a state of fury, demanding that God curse him if after his attack there was even one of Nabal's men left alive. When she heard that, Abigail got off her donkey and fell on her face before David, declaring herself his servant and pleading with him to call off the slaughter. "My Lord," she implored him, "let the blame be on me alone" (25:24).

How on earth could Abigail be to blame for Nabal's actions? Was she one of those wives who assume they are to blame for everything that goes wrong, even when they have no part in the matter? She knew better than to try to excuse Nabal this time, but perhaps she thought that shifting the blame to herself might placate David, who was obviously enraged. And she was wise to readily concede that her husband was a "wicked man" and a "fool" (25:25).

But Abigail went further than that and offered David a blessing, asking that God make his family a "lasting dynasty," that he be kept secure from his enemies, and that "no wrongdoing" would be found in him as long as he lived (25:28). This blessing so impressed David that he praised God for her and extended his hand in a gesture of peace.

When Abigail arrived home, she found Nabal drunk and carousing with his friends. So she waited until the following morning, after he had sobered up, to tell him about her peacemaking with David. Nabal promptly had a heart attack, went into a coma, and died ten days later.

How did such an intelligent and resourceful woman ever get hooked up with an abusive, drunken fool like Nabal in the first place? In an era of arranged marriages, of course, she probably did not have much choice in the matter. It is safe to say that she was not left a grieving widow. Now she was free of the tyranny of an alcoholic and abusive husband. She was liberated from the patriarchal constraints of an arranged marriage. She could relax and enjoy her newfound independence. But no, not Abigail. She immediately rushed into another marriage, this time a polygamous one with David, a man hardly known for his good relationships with women.

David's marriage proposal was apparently too tempting to turn down, so we find Abigail bowing down to David's servant, saying, "Here is your maidservant, ready to serve you and wash the feet of my master's servants" (25:41). This is an interesting reversal of position, considering the fact that Abigail was wealthy and David, at that time, was without resources.

We know little about the remainder of Abigail's life, except that she and David had a son named Kileab and that she was taken captive for a time by David's enemies. It seems, though, that she deserved better than the likes of Nabal and David.

We cannot, of course, impose our modern ideals and standards upon her time and culture. Yet in many ways, Abigail's story is very modern. It is all too common for smart women to make foolish choices in their relationships with men. Because marriage is such a high priority for many women, it is easy to make decisions of the heart without the necessary soul-searching and counsel.

Women need to see themselves as independent and complete without a man. This is as true for women in a good marriage as it is for single women. They need to have access to money and a means of support. In the event that her husband dies—or, God forbid, runs off with his secretary— a wife is then far better prepared to face life alone. No-fault divorce often leaves women stranded with no alimony and barely enough child support to make ends meet. Smart women will be prepared for such an eventuality.

But, some will ask, is it right to prepare for the possibility of a divorce? Many Christian counselors would argue that any woman who does is starting the marriage off on the wrong foot, paving the way for marital breakdown. The issue here is not an easy one. Of course a marriage must be built on trust, and if a women fears her husband will leave her for another woman she should not marry him in the first place.

But the matter really goes beyond this. Women are particularly vulnerable in marriage—and more so in divorce. Studies have shown that a woman's income decreases as much as seventy percent after a divorce, while a man's increases. Emotionally a husband may be just as distraught as his wife following a divorce, but financially he is generally in a far better position. For that reason, a wife needs to be as prepared as her husband should a death or divorce occur. In other words, she should be insured.

Acquiring death insurance (or *life* insurance, as we euphemistically refer to it) is a common practice. But divorce insurance is another matter. Because of our belief in the sanctity of the marriage vow, the very thought of this would rankle most Christians. Yet it makes sense. Is it right to insure your house for a fire? Of course. Most of us can't imagine living without homeowners' or renters' insurance, even though we go to extremes to prevent a catastrophe that would require its use. So, too, with divorce insurance. Divorce should be the very last thing we expect to happen in our marriage, and we ought to go to extremes to avoid a divorce, but we ought to be prepared nevertheless.

Just look around you in church next Sunday. How many in your congregation have had their homes burn down in recent years? Few if any, right? Now, how many in your congregation have broken marriages?

Divorce insurance is not the sort of thing a woman gets from her State Farm agent. No, divorce insurance is an attitude. It is an attitude of partnership in money and family business matters, so that in the event of death or divorce a wife is informed, up-to-date, and prepared and able to make decisions on her own. It is an attitude that subconsciously constrains a woman to keep up in her field of specialty, even if she has left her full-time career to be at home with young children.

I recently counseled a young woman with two small children on this very subject. She desperately wants her marriage to work, although she has already been through a short separation. The problems in her marriage are many, not the least of which are financial, including an unexpected call from the IRS with the shocking news that back taxes were owed for years when forms had not even been filed. Her husband had lied to her about the taxes and about his bonus income as well.

Among other things, I encouraged this otherwise bright and attractive and personable young woman to take over— or at least become actively involved in—the family finances. She had not wanted to make money a point of contention, but the recent tax problems proved that her husband could not be trusted. I also encouraged her to set aside the inheritance money that would be coming to her—perhaps to have her folks hold the money in their name. This obviously would not please her husband, who was aware of the inheritance, but I suggested she might simply tell him that she was setting the money aside for their retirement. This would certainly be the case, unless extenuating circumstances arose in the meantime.

Foolish choices in marriage are not exclusive to women. Many men also make foolish choices in marriage partners. But women, particularly Christian women, are much more likely to fall victim to this problem. If a wife turns out to be an abusive tyrant, at least she cannot inflict the misery under the guise of a biblical mandate—in fact, that can be turned against her. But no matter how dastardly the Christian husband may be, he can hide behind the dictum that the Christian husband is to be *head of the home.*

The story of Allison Hughes is a pathetic example of a smart woman making foolish choices. Allison told her story in her book *Love, Honor and Frustration,* which I first read a dozen years ago, and it was no less heartrending when I read it again recently. In the opening scene Allison, a middle-aged mother of four children, had pushed herself off a wooden dock into the black waters of Georgian Bay in an attempted suicide. She lived near the water in Shale Bay, Ontario, and had gone for a walk that night with no premeditation of suicide, but the longing for release almost seemed to pull her into the water. As the waves carried her further and further from the shore, the thought of not having to return home and face life comforted her.

It was the sound of her father's voice singing "Tell Me the Story of Jesus" deep in her childhood memories that finally forced her to swim back to the dock and climb out of the water, and that gave her the strength to go on.

Allison's childhood had been routine and happy. She was a farm girl who "loved to fork hay, shock grain, pick apples, and gather grapes," and she dreamed of one day becoming a missionary. An honor student who won awards in writing and athletics, she had a promising future. After college she was involved in church ministry—and then she married Harvey.

Allison and Harvey met at a church youth function, and their relationship grew over the next five years while she was in college and he was in the Army. Had she been more perceptive, she would have realized from the beginning that he was not the right mate for her. She was a go-getter and a visionary, excited about educational ministries at church and eager to expand her career as a writer, which soon got off to a promising start when she had a novel accepted for publication. Harvey, a shift worker (usually night shift) who spent his leisure time buying old motors at auctions and junkyards, insisted a woman's place was in the home, not at church socials or writers' conferences.

Prior to their marriage his opinion on the role of women was expressed primarily in biblical terminology. He would be the *head* of the home and she would *submit*. Their premarital counseling consisted of reading a book by John R. Rice, entitled *Home, Courtship, Marriage and Children*—which emphasized that only man, not woman, was created in the image of God, "So in the home, man is the deputy of God." Harvey gave a copy of that book to Allison on

Valentine's Day with all the passages on wifely submission underlined in red.

Not until six weeks after they were married did Allison suddenly see Harvey for the man he really was. It was a minor incident that would set the stage for the years that followed. Harvey was at the table with his face buried in the want ads as usual. Suddenly, "with the first forkful of food, he let out an explosion, half-roar and half-cry, spitting out a mouthful of food that spattered the dinner rolls and butter dish." It was cauliflower, Allison's favorite vegetable. She never fixed it again—at least not until after the healing that followed her suicide attempt.

Allison's response to Harvey's outburst tells as much about her as the outburst tells about him. Time and again she abandoned her own plans and desires to pacify him. She grew less involved in the church, and her once-successful writing career dwindled to nothing. When she planned a picnic with the children, Harvey insisted on eating his food at home. When she wanted to take the children Christmas shopping, he managed to thwart the plans. As the years went by Allison did her best to cook and clean and care for the children, finding her only escape in eating. As her self-image plummeted, her waistline expanded.

After her suicide attempt Allison began corresponding with a friend who challenged her to begin living her own life—to get back into church activities and her writing, and to lose the extra pounds she so despised. Allison did, but, feeling obligated to keep her "till death do us part" vows, she still had to endure Harvey. That endurance included giving in to his demands for his "marriage rights," as she recounts in her book:

> "Harvey, you're hurting me. Not like this. Harvey, love is not like this—"
>
> "How long do you think you can put me off, woman? How long do you think I'll go on supporting you without asserting my marriage rights?"

After that walk to the dock, the pastor advised Harvey, "Don't bother her for a while. She's had a shock. Let her get her strength back."

For a few weeks it was wonderful to go to bed without wondering if two hundred pounds of sweating man would wrestle the flesh until he felt he'd acted like a man, then flop over and snore loudly.

"What makes you think you're too good to act like a woman?"

"Harvey, if you want me to act like a woman at night, why don't you treat me like one during the day? You show more gentleness to the dog than you do to me. You bark out orders as if I were your slave. You couldn't treat a cleaning lady or garbage man the way you do me and expect them to go on working for you."

Silently I thought, *No wonder I've felt like a prostitute so often.* My dream of love, honor, and obey turned into a nightmare, "The Rape of the Cleaning Lady."

"You're so clever with words, you just call it whatever you want to." Deliberately he took his pink paycheck out of his back pocket, signed it, refolded it, and left it sticking out of his shirt pocket. "Now, are you going to come to bed and do your duty as a wife, or aren't you?"

"Do I have any choice?" I asked. . . .

In the morning when I found Harvey's check where he'd tossed it on the kitchen counter, I wept. Not for myself, but for Harvey. . . .[1]

As I thought about her again when I began writing this book, I wondered what had happened to Allison Hughes since 1977 when her book was published. I decided to do a little investigating, but tracking her down was not easy. "Allison Hughes" was a pen name, and her publisher had not had any correspondence from her since 1978. After making a number of phone calls, I finally reached her married son, who told me his mother had died in 1988 at the age of sixty-three after a long bout with cancer.

I feared he might be irritated by this stranger on the other end of the line asking personal questions about his parents, but he was not. He obviously cared deeply about his mother and wanted to talk. He told me that his father never knew about the book until just before his mother died, when she told him and requested that he not read it. He did anyway and was, to say the least, not thrilled with it. He has since remarried, to a woman more suited to his "legalistic fundamentalism."

"Mom was open-minded, kind of a freethinker," recalled her son, "and her creative bent just didn't mesh with Dad's interests."

As we talked, I learned that the family has done okay. There are problems, as in all families, but God has blessed them despite the difficulties. We talked for ten or fifteen minutes, a most pleasant conversation. The son of Allison and Harvey was a very caring and gentle man.

In their intense longing for marriage and family, many women make foolish choices. Allison Hughes is a vivid reminder that even the smartest of women are vulnerable. And not just *young* women. Many women today are past their mid-twenties before they marry, but too often their choices do not reflect a comparable maturity. And those who marry a second or third time, following either widowhood or divorce, are usually much older than that. And the evidence indicates that these women are even more likely to make foolish choices.

How do we avoid making foolish choices in the area of our love lives? We tend to think of love as a very private matter and that a woman's taste in men is very personal. But we need to get away from this kind of individualistic thinking. When it comes to something as serious as marriage, we desperately need the advice and counsel of others, especially family and friends. If they are questioning our choice, then so ought we. We must ever remind ourselves that, indeed, love is blind and can almost be a disabling disease when it comes to decision making. We must proceed with caution.

Had Allison analyzed Harvey more during their courtship, looking at him realistically, she would have seen the warning signs. She should have asked herself what she wanted in marriage—what she wanted in a love relationship. And she should have asked some hard questions. We must also ask *ourselves* some very basic questions:

- Why am I attracted to him? Deep down, do I have a desire to "mother" him—to help solve his problems? Am I looking for someone to take care of me, to solve my problems and protect me from a cruel world?
- Am I looking for love that was not freely given me as a child? Am I afraid to go through life without a man?
- Am I worried about being an "old maid" or concerned about what other people think about the fact that I'm *still* single?
- Am I dissatisfied with the way he is now? Do I think I can change him after we are married?
- Who are his friends? How does he treat his mother? His sisters? What is his basic view of women?
- What does he do in his leisure time? How does he spend his money? Is he generous or stingy?
- What is the depth of his spirituality? Is he given to proof-texting and pious platitudes? Is he genuinely concerned about spiritual growth?

Such inquiries hardly qualify as in-depth analysis, but even this much would have alerted Allison to potential problems with Harvey. By seriously contemplating these questions and answering them honestly, we can avoid the foolish choices that are so often the undoing of smart women.

Who, then, are the smart women who make wise choices? The two male clinical psychologists who authored the book *Smart Women, Foolish Choices* give a profile from a secular perspective, but most of it can be appropriately blended into a Christian perspective:

> The smart woman knows she is responsible for her experience in this world. She refuses to be a victim. She works hard at getting what she wants and needs. . . . She has learned to communicate her needs early in the relationship, and if she sees the match as not fulfilling, she moves on. She doesn't hang on to misery or empty promises. . . . She doesn't expect perfection in a man or in herself. She can join with a man fully and with the total expression of her personality. But she never makes a man the center of her existence. . . . The smart woman embraces her femininity and sexuality. . . . It is not a role she puts on; it is a manifestation of her freedom and trust in the pleasure of being a woman and feeling womanly.[2]

Are smart women who make foolish choices failures? No. It is reassuring to know that smart women who make foolish choices can turn their lives around and actually become very successful in the process. Even Allison made progress. She still had to endure Harvey, who never changed, but she got control of her own life and was also able to fashion her story into a fascinating book that has served to warn other women.

Another woman who stands as an extraordinary example of a survivor of foolish choices is Dorothy Sayers. She was a remarkably talented woman, a critically acclaimed and popular author and lecturer. But the public facade concealed a troubled private life from those who clamored to hear her speak or to read her books and essays. Her personal letters reveal, among other things, "her love affairs, her tragic marriage to an alcoholic ne'er-do-well, the birth of her illegitimate child." Yet God used her in a remarkable way in spite of her foolish choices.[3]

There is hope and redemption for women from even the most foolish of choices. By all counts Allison's decision to marry Harvey was not a wise one. Yet that marriage produced four children who brought her joy—children who, with their mother's encouragement and prayers, determined to rise above their dysfunctional family.

But the ideal in living out God's will is to avoid foolish choices, particularly those choices that are blinded by love, including that most crucial choice of a marriage partner. Paul warns us of this just before he focuses on husband/wife relationships in Ephesians 5: "Be very careful, then, how you live—not as unwise but as wise, making the most of every opportunity, because the days are evil. Therefore do not be foolish, but understand what the Lord's will is" (Eph. 5:15–17).

Allison made a foolish choice in her failure to discern the will of God in marriage, but it was Harvey who blatantly misinterpreted God's Word for his own purposes. When he gave Allison a book on marriage with the passages on submission underlined in red, he was deliberately disregarding Paul's emphatic admonition to husbands. Had he heeded that admonition and loved Allison as "Christ loved the church and gave himself up for her," their marriage would have been entirely different.

No husband can fully live up to the ideal in Ephesians 5—nor can a wife. But it is nevertheless a standard by which all marriages should be characterized—one that challenges both partners to seek to surpass the other in creatively designing their garden of love.

The garden of love is supposed to be an idyllic setting, but all too often it is just the opposite. For women like Allison, the joys and desires of love and marriage are marred by "Thou shalt nots," and the garden itself is darkened by the shadows of the tombstones of those, like her, who have made foolish choices.

I went to the Garden of Love
And saw what I never had seen:

A Chapel was built in the midst,
Where I used to play on the green.

And the gates of the Chapel were shut,
And "Thou shalt not" writ over the door;
So I turned to the Garden of Love
That so many sweet flowers bore;

And I saw it was filled with graves
And tomb-stones where flowers should be;
And priests in black gowns were walking their rounds,
And binding with briars my joys and desires.

                        —William Blake
                Songs of Experience *(1794)*

Nine

Manipulative Choices

Rebekah's manipulative choice to promote her favorite son Jacob was: (a) *no worse than Isaac's deceptive scheme to present her as his sister,* (b) *vindicated in the end because it was Jacob, not Esau, whom God used for his plan for Israel,* (c) *as evil as any other sins committed by God's people,* (d) *not commendable, but necessary to accomplish her goals.*

*R*ebekah lived in a patriarchal, polygamous society where women were bound by law and custom to accept their inferior status. Both she and her mother-in-law Sarah knew firsthand the humiliation of being treated as sex objects, even by their own husbands.

How must Rebekah have felt when she and her husband, Isaac, were guests of the Philistine King Abimelech, and Isaac spread the word that she was his sister in order to protect himself? Isaac knew all too well that the beautiful Rebekah would be considered a real prize for the king or one of his deputies, who knew better than to ravish a married woman—unless, of course, their hormones drove them to conspire to kill Isaac and then take his wife. So the solution was easy: just introduce her as his sister, and if they ravished her, so be it; at least he would be out of danger.

Did Rebekah have any say in the matter? Did she have any rights over her own body? Not in the eyes of her husband and certainly not in the eyes of the king—at least it doesn't seem so from the way he worded his angry question to Isaac: "What is this you have done to us? One of the men might well have slept with your wife, and you would have brought guilt upon us" (Gen. 26:10). Isaac surely must have known the potential danger to Rebekah, but his own security was more important to him.

Even in the hundreds of generations since her death, Rebekah has not been able to escape the discriminatory affronts to her gender—no longer made by a husband and a king, but by commentators and Bible scholars. One writer, in discussing her arranged marriage at age twenty, commends her "childlike simplicity." Yet the biblical account gives no indication of this. Indeed, a straightforward reading of the text gives the impression that Rebekah was a very mature and hospitable young woman who single-handedly supervised the reception of an entire caravan of strangers.[1]

But the Rebekah we know best is the middle-aged, manipulative mother of two sons—a strong, forceful woman who had learned how to circumvent the obstacles of sex discrimination. Society might dictate that her husband was the head of the household, but she wielded the real power in the family, and she used that power to promote the welfare of her favorite son, Jacob.

Rebekah was bound and determined that Jacob should receive the birthright blessing and inheritance that rightfully belonged to his elder brother, Esau. So driven was she that she concocted a disguise for Jacob that would have been more appropriate for a Halloween costume party than a private family religious rite. But it worked, and that was what mattered to Rebekah. Isaac suspected something was wrong, but he went ahead with the blessing. He was old and blind and perhaps well into the first stages of Alzheimer's disease.

It would be easy to rationalize Rebekah's behavior in light of her culture. As a woman she had been unfairly treated, and this was her only recourse. Why should she have been excluded from the giving of the blessing? Was not her opinion just as valid as her husband's? If so, how else could she accomplish her objective? It is often easier to be manipulative and deceptive than to be straightforward and direct, especially for women in a culture or community of faith that frowns on strong-minded females.

Rebekah's behavior might also be rationalized because her intention was well-founded. Jacob was more deserving of the blessing. Why shouldn't she help him, especially if he was willing to go along with the playacting? In one sense Rebekah was history's first stage mother. She did everything in her power to set up her child to beat out the competition, even if it required collusion and deception.

It never ceases to amaze me how far some mothers are willing to go to promote their children or make their children fulfill their own dreams. I'm sure there are also stage fathers—perhaps more often sports fathers—but there seems to be something in the female psyche that makes women more vulnerable to this kind of manipulation.

The ultimate stage mother story came out of Texas in 1991. According to *Time* magazine, "Wanda Webb Holloway, organist at the local Baptist church, is an irrepressible stage mother." So desperate was she for her daughter to become a cheerleader at the local junior high school that she allegedly plotted to have the mother of her daughter's rival murdered by a hit man. It was not the first time this stage mother had interfered in her daughter's competition. Two years earlier she had tried to get the same girl disqualified on the basis of a technicality, and the following year Wanda's own daughter was disqualified because Holloway distributed pencils and rulers promoting her.

What a pitiful story of an obviously sick woman. But what was even more troubling were the reflections of the apparently sane principal of the school: "After all, it's the American way. We all want our children to achieve. There is a part of Wanda Holloway in all of us."[2]

Can we really dismiss such behavior so lightly? I hope not.

Manipulation comes in many forms, stage mothers being only one variety. Many women feel trapped in a marriage or by a society that is stacked against them. But whatever the degree of manipulation, it is wrong, and in the end we pay for it. Proverbs 14 is explicit on this point:

> The wise woman builds her house, but with her own hands the foolish one tears hers down.
> He whose walk is upright fears the Lord, but he whose ways are devious despises him.
> A truthful witness does not deceive, but a false witness pours out lies.
> The wisdom of the prudent is to give thought to their ways, but the folly of fools is deception.
> Do not those who plot evil go astray? But those who plan what is good find love and faithfulness (14:1, 2, 5, 8, 22).

One of the most insidious forms of manipulation that has become all too common in recent years is the fabricated testimony. I first became aware of this deceitful trend more than a decade ago when I was teaching a course on Christian biography and had included on my recommended reading list the book *Crying Wind*, the story of a Native American woman who had endured incredible hardship before she committed her life to Christ. Students read it and were inspired by it. Only later did we all learn that much of what the author had written was untrue.

The same can be said for the testimony of Nora Lam, whose story has been widely publicized through the book and film *China Cry*. Here she gives an "unbelievable" account of escaping the terrors of the Chinese communists. But a background check of Lam and her circumstances convinced John Stewart, a Christian radio talk show host, not to endorse the film: "Based on my interviews with numerous people who've known Nora Lam, I've reluctantly come to the conclusion that her stories simply aren't credible."³

And then there is Betty Malz, whose best-selling book, *My Glimpse of Eternity*, detailing her experience of being clinically dead, has been disavowed by her doctors. Malz claims that "surgery revealed that I had suffered a ruptured appendix eleven days before, and that gangrene had coated all of my organs, causing them to disintegrate." She then goes on to say: "Early one morning, after I had hung on in a coma for 44 days, the night nurse on the third floor came to check my vital signs and found no response. I had slipped from this life into the next. At five A.M. a doctor pronounced me clinically dead, pulled a sheet over my head, and left the room in darkness." After that Malz went to heaven, where she remained until her father, who arrived on the scene twenty-eight minutes later, brought her back to earth.

It is this story, more than anything else, that has thrust Malz into the limelight, and the story has been repeated in each of her six books and told time and again at the various women's conferences where she is the featured speaker.

But according to Dr. Henry Bopp, Malz's doctor, "her story is almost a complete fabrication." It is true that she was in the hospital, but only for twenty-nine days—not enough to account for her forty-four-day coma. Indeed, hospital records show she was released on the date of her supposed death. "She did not die," says Bopp. "She may have dreamt she did, but she did not die in the hospital."⁴

Some would argue that these testimonies have inspired millions of Christians and non-Christians alike, and that any prevarication, while not commendable, has been essentially harmless. Like Rebekah, they reason that the manipulation is for a good cause. The end justifies the means.

But truth is not something we can compromise. Dishonest, manipulative choices are wrong choices.

Even more pernicious is that genre that flourishes on contrived testimonies as well as lurid accusations of others. These books feature sensational stories of satanic rituals or sexual abuse—or both. Lauren Stratford, a professing evangelical Christian who has told her story in *Satan's Underground*, is a prime example of this.

According to Lauren, from the time she was a small child she was physically and sexually abused by pornographers hired by her mother. This led to her forced involvement in Satanism as a young adult, during which time she gave birth to three babies, two of whom were killed in "snuff" films and the third in a satanic ritual. This nightmare allegedly ended through the help of a therapist and contact with Hal Lindsey and his sister-in-law, Johanna Michaelsen, a well-known author who has written on evil and the occult. It was through their help that her story was published in book form.

No one should doubt the possibility of such a scenario, but neither should one assume it is true without verification. When someone is accused of shoplifting, we demand proof; certainly no less should be required when accusing people of satanic ritual abuse. But in Christian circles we are incredibly gullible when it comes to sensational testimonies.

Friends and relatives of Lauren say her real story is very different than the one that brought her rewarding publicity. According to Lauren's sister, their parents were devout Christians, and "there was no place in our home for anything remotely occultic or pornographic." There were family problems, but nothing resembling what Lauren described in her book. In high school and college she had accused individuals of sexually abusing her. Later she admitted to making up some of these stories to "impress" friends. On numerous occasions she cut her wrists and arms in attention-getting suicide attempts and at one point claimed blindness, which she later conceded was faked.

Despite her claims of sacrificing her babies soon after she had given birth, there is no evidence that she ever had any children. Yet with no supporting evidence she was able to find many people who were eager to believe her.

For Lauren Stratford manipulative choices came easy. With the aid of her well-placed friends she caught the attention of a publisher by offering a book that promised high sales and wide publicity. She was featured on the "700 Club" and interviewed by Geraldo. Even Oprah Winfrey recognized the publicity value of her sensationalized story and invited her on as a guest. On network television, Lauren, the professing Christian, gained the sympathetic ear of the talk-show host, with the only serious challenge coming from another guest, Michael Aquino, the founder of a satanic church known as the Temple of Set.

Fortunately, Bob and Gretchen Passantino, a husband-wife cult research team from California, and Jon Trott of *Cornerstone* magazine, launched a painstaking investigation of Lauren's life. In dozens of interviews, relatives, friends, school officials, and her pastor told of a long trail of lies and deceptions that showed Lauren was a victim only in her own imagination. The result of their work was an award-winning article that gave a picture of a deeply troubled woman and prompted her publisher to pull the book off the market—but not before more than a hundred and thirty thousand copies had been sold.[5]

The story of Lauren Stratford ought to be a lesson and a warning. But this problem is not restricted to writers and public speakers. There is a tendency in all of us to manipulate the truth for our own benefit and to zealously and unquestioningly propagate the claims of others when they suit our purposes. At one time or another all of us can be tempted to exaggerate, to embellish—to make ourselves more appealing or our stories more exciting.

Isobel Kuhn, a missionary with the China Inland Mission

for many years, has been a model for me in this area. She has admitted her weakness and deals with it openly and honestly. In her autobiography she tells about her ability to write creative missionary letters to supporters back home. The only problem with them was their inaccuracy. When her husband challenged the veracity of many of her stories, insisting that she had embellished some of them beyond the point of recognition, she resented his criticism, but she was at the same time convicted. Taking his pointed admonitions to heart, she allowed them to better equip her to be the best-selling missionary author she would later become.

"God was preparing to use my pen in relating stories of His work in human hearts," she writes. "I couldn't afford to let that pen grow careless as to facts. . . . a Christian writer can't be too particular that every point be according to reality."[6]

Manipulating the truth and manipulating people often go together. Both involve deception for personal gratification and attention that may be otherwise denied the individual. The more exploited a woman is, the more likely she is to be manipulative. Sometimes she may appear satisfied on the surface while inside she is angry and bitter. Indeed, some of the most vigorous advocates of wifely submission are women who, behind the scenes, are actually very controlling. Some are unaware that they are using this twisted mode of attaining power, but often it is a purposeful scheme, like Rebekah's, to win their desired aims.

The martyr complex is another form of manipulation at which wives and mothers can be very adept. Sacrificing all for husband and children, these women neglect themselves while allowing resentment and hostility to build. In the end this attitude only facilitates dysfunctional family living, as Anne Wilson Schaef explains in her description of the "Good Christian Martyr."

The Good Christian Martyr releases her rage through sacrifice and suffering. She always takes the smallest piece of meat at mealtime. If there is not enough dessert to go around, she does without. She never buys any clothes for herself because she is not important, but she always makes sure that her children and her husband have new clothes. She gains control over others by inducing guilt. She is perhaps the most manipulative and powerful of all angry women. Some of the most damaged women I have worked with in therapy are those who have had Good Christian Martyr mothers. They try but they can never live up to the image of their perfect mothers who sacrificed so much.[7]

The "total woman" philosophy of two decades ago was another form of manipulation in which wives were encouraged to dress up in costumes and become playthings for their husbands. "Never let him know what to expect when he opens the front door; make it like opening a surprise package. You may be a smoldering sexpot, or an all-American fresh beauty. Be a pixie or a pirate—a cowgirl or a show girl. Keep him off guard."[8] Such advice sounds outlandish, but for many women of the 1970s it seemed an innovative way to attain what they wanted without having to be straightforward and sincere.

An even more manipulative formula came from Helen B. Andelin in her book *Fascinating Womanhood* when she counseled women to be childlike in order to achieve the desired results. For example, she suggested, wives should become "adorably angry" and throw childlike tantrums to get their way. "This extreme girlishness makes him feel in contrast, stronger, and so much more of a man." But there is nothing genuine here. "The key to childlike anger is this: your anger, your sauciness, or spunk must be mostly pretense." What is the objective of this phoney display? "When he realizes . . . your helpless dependency upon him, he is psychologically in a position to do the utmost to fulfill your requests."[9]

Manipulation used to *get* a man is just as repugnant as that used to *keep* him. Yet single women longing for marriage are sometimes tempted to use manipulative techniques to accomplish their goals. The Bible is not silent on the subject of women who sought to manipulate men in love relationships. Two of the most notorious were Delilah and the unnamed hussy known only as Potiphar's wife, the married woman who sought to seduce Joseph.

There was nothing subtle about Potiphar's wife, who lusted for the "well-built and handsome" young Hebrew. "Come to bed with me!" she boldly summoned. He refused, but she persisted: "Though she spoke to Joseph day after day, he refused to go to bed with her or even be with her." How did she dare treat him in such a manner? The answer is simple. She had power. She was the matron of an Egyptian mansion, wife of the Pharaoh's captain of the guard, and Joseph was nothing more than a slave, even though he had been given great responsibility by his master. So this scheming woman used her position to manipulate Joseph, and when that did not work she sought to ruin him by accusing him of trying to seduce her (Gen. 39:1–20).

Delilah, whose story is told in Judges 16, was much more subtle. Using her beauty and seductive allurement, she practiced her manipulative wiles on Samson, whom I would characterize as a primitive version (if that's possible) of Hulk Hogan. Though ruled more by his hormones than his IQ, Samson led Israel for a number of years during the time of the Judges and managed to plague the Philistines with his amazing strength and his macho demeanor.

Delilah was an undercover agent for the Philistines, and her assignment was to literally work under the covers. Through her sexual prowess she manipulated Samson into revealing the secret of his strength.

Three times Samson gave her the wrong answer, and three times, like clockwork, he was attacked by Philistine thugs, only to prove that they had not discovered his secret. I've sometimes wondered why, if Samson actually had an IQ above 75, he didn't simply give up on Delilah, but apparently she knew well the art of manipulation. So on the fourth try he ended up telling her the secret of his long hair, and she very predictably called in the thugs to cut it, and Samson lost his strength. And we all know the rest of the story—of Samson, that is. As for Delilah, she is never heard from again in the Bible. Where was she? Probably off on a new assignment with some other marginally coherent hunk.

These extreme examples of manipulation by scheming women may not appear to have any relevance to us, but I think they do. When we find ourselves left outside the power structures and excluded from the board rooms where the "good old boys" make the decisions that keep the world going, it is sometimes tempting to use whatever means we have to gain entrance, gain power, and gain control—more specifically, control over men. But this is not the way of Christ.

Sometimes it is difficult to draw the line between choices that are perceptive and shrewd and those that are calculating and manipulative. But as is true in most choices we make, motivation is the key. It is imperative that we be astute both in the ways of the world and in our Christian walk, but we must always guard our motives. Indeed, we need to check our motives to make sure our decision making is not flawed by manipulative choices.

- Do I strive to control others—especially in subtle ways? Am I not satisfied unless I get my own way?
- Is there a sense of drivenness in my desire to succeed, or to make my loved ones succeed? Am I a "stage mother" in my own unique way?
- Do I connive and conspire to outsmart others? Am I secretly pleased when others fail—especially when it serves my purposes?

- Am I loose with the truth? Do I exaggerate to make myself or those I love more appealing or successful?
- Do I feel helpless in a society or family situation that discriminates against women, convincing me that manipulation or a martyr complex is my only viable solution?
- Am I able to admit my tendency—a nearly universal one—to be manipulative?

Answering this last question in the affirmative is our first step to moving beyond manipulative choices. Sometimes it is a valuable exercise to reflect on our relationships with each of our close family members, friends, and coworkers, and to think hard about how we might have been manipulative in any of these relationships. Then we should commit ourselves to avoiding that form of control in the future.

Jesus proclaimed a timeless principle when he admonished his followers to be "wise as serpents, and harmless as doves" (Matt. 10:16 KJV). In other words, be crafty and shrewd, as long as it is accompanied by a spirit of benevolence and goodwill.

As women, we need to take this admonition seriously. Often it seems that the deck is stacked against us and that we have no choice but to manipulate. Yet we must resist the kind of relentless determination that drove Rebekah to prevail no matter what. When Jacob protested against his mother's manipulative scheme, saying that it could result in a *curse* rather than a blessing, she impulsively uttered those unforgettable words: "Let the curse fall on me. Just do what I say" (Gen. 27:13).

For Rebekah, manipulation brought only added turmoil and heartache. When she heard that her son Esau was threatening to kill his brother Jacob as soon as their father Isaac died, she panicked and sent her favorite son off to live with his uncle. When we see Rebekah for the last time, she is muttering to Isaac that she could not bear to go on living if Jacob were to marry one of those awful Hittite women (Gen. 27:46). We don't know how bad these women really were, but some of us might say to Rebekah, "You're a fine one to judge them!"

Manipulative choices have a way of corrupting our moral senses. One choice leads to another and then to another, and soon the course of action becomes a way of life, though often hidden under the guise of "getting what we rightfully deserve." And the irony of it all is, that in the end, we probably do.

> *We get back our mete as we measure;*
> *We cannot do wrong and feel right;*
> *Nor can we give pain and gain pleasure*
> *For justice avenges each slight.*
> *The air for the wing of the sparrow,*
> *The bush for the robin and wren,*
> *But always the path that is narrow*
> *And strait for the children of men.*
> —*Alice Cary (1820–71)*

Ten

Painful Choices

Hannah's decision to leave Samuel at the temple when he was six years old reflects: **(a)** *a blatant case of child neglect,* **(b)** *a woman's utter devotion to God,* **(c)** *remarkable courage and strength of character,* **(d)** *an intense suppression of maternal instincts.*

Hannah is an enigma to me. How could she abandon her son at the temple? It boggles my mind. But then so does Abraham in his willingness to slay his son Isaac as a sacrifice to God. In both instances it was a matter of obedience to God, but I still struggle with the reality of both situations. If I had been faced with such painful choices, I think I would have rationalized that I had somehow misunderstood God. Surely he couldn't have meant what he said—or what I *thought* he said.

Hannah's story is a pathetic one that was almost swallowed up by her apparent problem of infertility. More than anything else in the world she wanted a baby. More specifically, she wanted a son. Her husband, Elkanah, shared her pain and showered her with love and favors, but he simply did not understand her feelings, nor did he know how to deal with his depressed wife. His questions show his frustration: "Hannah, why are you weeping? Why don't you eat? Why are you downhearted? Don't I mean more to you than ten sons?" (1 Sam. 1:8).

Adding to his frustration was the fact that he could not prevent his second wife, Peninnah, who had children galore,

from making life miserable for Hannah. Peninnah saw
Hannah as "her rival" and "kept provoking her in order to
irritate her." This "went on year after year" (1 Sam. 1:6–7).

Hannah had only one recourse left: to relinquish her
heartbreak to God and trust him for the ultimate favor he
could bestow on her. The temple was the appropriate
setting for this spiritual encounter, and during their annual
pilgrimage to this holy place, Hannah poured out her heart
to God. "In bitterness of soul Hannah wept much and
prayed to the LORD" (1 Sam. 1:10). God was her only
recourse, because, as the Scripture tells us, "the LORD had
closed her womb" (1 Sam. 1:5).

Eli, the priest, "sitting on a chair by the doorpost of the
LORD's temple," did not even recognize the fact that
Hannah was agonizing in prayer (1 Sam. 1:9). He thought
she was drunk. (Imagine having him for a pastor. He
wouldn't have recognized true spirituality if it had hit him in
the face!)

When he accused Hannah of being drunk and ordered
her to get rid of her wine (did he think she had a wine skin
tucked under her skirt?), she didn't even bother explaining
the cause of her anguish and grief. She did, however, stifle
her sobs long enough to respond to his outrageous accusa-
tion, and in a remarkably charitable manner: "Not so, my
lord . . . I am a woman who is deeply troubled. I have not
been drinking wine or beer; I was pouring out my soul to
the LORD" (1 Sam. 1:15).

I've always been in awe of her response. I think I would
have shoved the old geezer off his chair by the doorpost and
stormed out. But Hannah's response paid off. Eli, perhaps
to make up for his faux pas, blessed her with a prophetic
blessing: "Go in peace, and may the God of Israel grant you
what you have asked him" (1 Sam. 1:17). And God did just
that: baby Samuel was born to Hannah and Elkanah.

Part of me can identify with Hannah, but a large part of

me cannot. I have never endured the anguish of being infertile, but I have given birth to a son—an only son—an only child. I know the incredible torrent of love that surges from a mother's breast—that potent protectiveness of a mother for a child. I can understand how Hannah might be haunted by a vow she made to God, but I cannot understand how could she take that little boy as soon as he was weaned and leave him with Eli, a man who couldn't even control his own sons.

No, I can't identify with her in that, but I am willing to concede that her level of spirituality was far beyond mine. Unlike most of us, Hannah recognized that she owed everything to God: God had made her barren and God had made her fertile. For her, there was never any question of breaking her promise to him.

Hannah made a painful choice, but she was able to make it because she trusted God. That is the crux of the matter— something that ought to cause us all to do some real soul-searching. Can we really trust God in the painful choices? We must. Because the fact of the matter is that the right choices are often painful choices.

Today the temptation is to avoid pain at all costs. We are a society of escapists, and Christians are not immune. We go on shopping sprees to avoid depression (remember Tammy Faye Bakker?). We use our credit cards to buy pleasure, and then go deeper into debt to pay our credit card bills, unwilling to make the painful choices required to free ourselves from debt. During the 1980s—the decade of excess—our whole country avoided painful choices, thus shamelessly bequeathing even more painful choices to a future generation. Painful choices are not popular choices, but they are a necessary part of the decision making of life.

Painful choices have not always been so out of style among Christians. During medieval times, when asceticism was in vogue, it was common for holy women (and men) to wear hair shirts, to roll in prickly nettles, and in at least one instance to pull out perfectly good teeth, believing that such efforts pleased God. Such misguided spirituality is not the sort of painful choice God wants us to make. Yet it does point to a time when personal well-being and comfort were not the highest on the believer's list of priorities.

Today the pendulum has swung the other way. We are unwilling to make any sacrifice that would cause discomfort. We endure pain when we have no other choice, but we seldom intentionally make painful choices. This was not so in the early church. Both Paul and Peter not only warned that believers would face pain and suffering, but also challenged them (and us) to be willing to endure death, if that was the cost of discipleship.

To the Philippians Paul wrote, "For it has been granted to you on behalf of Christ not only to believe on him, but also to suffer for him" (Phil. 1:29). Even as our believing involves a volitional choice, so does our suffering. When state-sponsored persecution imperiled the lives and livelihoods of Christians in the early centuries, they *chose* to suffer rather than deny the faith. They were spiritually conditioned for painful choices—a conditioning we have lost in our overindulgent contemporary church.

Pain is a choice—a right choice—in certain situations and for certain benefits. "Everyone who wants to live a godly life in Christ Jesus," wrote Paul, "will be persecuted" (2 Tim. 3:12). We can avoid the persecution and the pain, but not without paying a price. Moses, according to the writer of the Hebrews, "chose to be mistreated along with the people of God rather than to enjoy the pleasures of sin for a short time. He regarded disgrace for the sake of Christ as of greater value than the treasures of Egypt, because he was looking ahead to his reward" (Heb. 11:25–26).

Normally we think of painful choices as those decisions that are beneficial to others or to the kingdom of God as a whole, failing to recognize the benefit they have in our own lives, especially in the area of character building. The classic passage on character in Romans speaks to this: "We also rejoice in our sufferings, because we know that suffering produces perseverance; perseverance, character; and character, hope" (Rom. 5:3–4).

M. Scott Peck, a well-known psychiatrist, writes of character-building problems and painful choices in his book *The Road Less Traveled*:

> Problems are the cutting edge that distinguishes between success and failure. Problems call forth our courage and our wisdom; indeed, they create our courage and our wisdom. It is only because of problems that we grow mentally and spiritually. When we desire to encourage the growth of the human spirit, we challenge and encourage the human capacity to solve problems, just as in school we deliberately set problems for our children to solve. It is through the pain of confronting and resolving problems that we learn. As Benjamin Franklin said, "Those things that hurt, instruct." It is for this reason that wise people learn not to dread but actually to welcome problems and actually to welcome the pain of problems.
>
> Most of us are not so wise. Fearing the pain involved, almost all of us, to a greater or lesser degree, attempt to avoid problems. We procrastinate, hoping that they will go away. We ignore them, forget them, pretend they do not exist. We even take drugs to assist us in ignoring them, so that by deadening ourselves to the pain we can forget the problems that cause the pain. We attempt to skirt around problems rather than meet them head on. We attempt to get out of them rather than suffer through them.[1]

We must be careful, though, that we are not wrongly motivated in our painful choices. Women, especially those who are mothers, are prone to make choices based on a martyr-complex mentality that says, "Everyone else comes first, and I'll suffer in silence for the sake of my family." But it is often this very attitude that festers beneath the surface, long after the choice is made, and causes growing resent-ment.

At every stage of our lives we face painful choices. One that is particularly common among young women is the breakup of a dating relationship. Despite our feelings of love and our longing for marriage, the relationship for one reason or another must end. How much more painful this is when the realization comes only weeks or days or even hours before the wedding.

I recently talked to a friend who is divorcing her husband after thirteen years of marriage. She confessed that she realized beyond a shadow of a doubt on the day before her wedding that her fiancé was not the right one for her, but the thought of calling off the wedding at that late hour was just too painful. Yet she would have spared herself thirteen years of abuse and unhappiness had she gritted her teeth and made that painful, embarrassing choice.

Or take the case of Kerry, an attractive seminary student of mine. God had called Kerry into foreign missions, but she had fallen in love with a fellow who was headed for a secular vocation. Missions held no interest for him, and he had hoped that Kerry would grow out of her single-minded commitment. Kerry, in turn, had prayed that God would call her boyfriend into missions. It didn't happen, and she resolutely made the painful choice to end the relationship. I reminded her of great missionary women such as Lottie Moon, Mary Slessor, and Lillian Trasher who had made similar choices, but it did little to ease the pain she was feeling at that moment.

Unwanted pregnancies also demand painful choices—sometimes wrong choices and sometimes right ones. How painful, and yet how right, when a pregnant, unwed teenager chooses to give her baby to a married couple who desperately wants a child. How painful, and yet how wrong, when a pregnant, unwed teenager chooses to have an abortion. There is a temptation in our quick-fix culture to think that an abortion is only temporarily painful, but countless testimonies confirm the heartrending, persistent pain suffered by those who have used the creed of pro-choice for a wrong choice.

Even wanted children can be the cause of painful choices later in their lives. How devastating it is for parents to face the painful decisions involved when their children are swept into the sins of substance abuse, promiscuity, or criminal activity. Tough love must prevail, despite the pain. Sometimes parents must send their children to a rehabilitation center, or even kick them out.

But if children can be the cause of painful choices, so can parents. I'll never forget the summer I took my eighty-two-year-old father to check out a small group home for elderly adults who were unable to live on their own. He wanted no part of it. He had lived on his farm for fifty years and was resisting every suggestion of alternative living. In the end it was not his choice when he moved from his farm to a local nursing home. It was a painful choice for his five children—a painful choice that turned out to be a right choice and a happy choice for my father.

But there were more painful choices to come. At the age of eighty-nine my father's health and quality of life had deteriorated to the point where we longed for his passing. When his doctor suggested terminating a course of medical treatment, four of us concurred. We did not want our father to linger on for months in pain. But my younger brother opposed the decision. I'm thankful that the Lord took the painful choice out of our hands, for in a matter of weeks Dad was gone.

The real test is not how high we rate the degree of pain a particular choice brings, but how well we rise to the challenge of making that choice and carrying through on it. For example, once Hannah had decided to fulfill her vow to

God, no matter how painful, she did so without allowing it to destroy her.

A twentieth-century version of Hannah is seen in the life of Evelyn Brand. The year was 1923. Evelyn and her husband, Jesse, had served as missionaries in India for ten years and were on furlough back in England. It should have been an exciting time for Evelyn, not having seen her family and friends for so long. But the year was both a blessing and a torture, writes her biographer, for when Evelyn and Jesse returned to India, their eight-year-old son Paul and six-year-old daughter Connie would be staying in England to be properly educated.

"As the sands of the year ran low the constant dread of parting turned into agony" for Evelyn. To be separated from her children for several years was a choice that was just too painful.

> "I can't do it," she blurted suddenly to Jesse about a month before they were due to sail. "Paul, yes. He's old enough to stand the separation, and he must have his schooling now. But Connie, my little darling . . . Jess, I must take her."
>
> Jesse's face reflected the pain in her own, but he shook his head. "I know. But, my dear, it would be cruel to separate them." Then, looking into her ravaged eyes, he relented. "Very well. Why not take Connie apart and ask her if she would rather go back with us?"
>
> Evie thankfully grasped at the thread of hope. Connie regarded her gravely. "Can Paul come too, Mummy?"
>
> "No, darling. Paul must stay here and go to school."
>
> The child shook her head. "Oh, not without Paul, Mummy. Not without my Paul."

The painful choice had been made for Evelyn, but it didn't make the outcome any easier. The agonizing dread and anguish during those last few weeks was nothing short of torment: the grief of separation combined with the haunting fear that this painful choice might be the wrong choice. When the day of departure arrived, they said their good-byes in the morning before Connie and Paul headed out the door for school. "Evie stood by the gate looking after them, eyes so blurred with tears she could scarcely see the waving of their hands before they ran around the corner." The pain was indescribable, as Evelyn later confessed: "As I stood watching them, something just died in me."[2]

The years of separation were difficult for both Evelyn and the children, climaxed by the sorrow of losing Jesse, their husband and father. When Evelyn saw her children again, six years later, fifteen-year-old Paul was hardly recognizable. Nor was she. His mother had become, as Paul described her, "a little, shrunken old lady!" Yet Evelyn and her children savored their time together, knowing that she would be returning to India the following year, leaving them for another five years.

As a mother I have misgivings about the choice Evelyn Brand made. Is it right to bring children into the world and then abandon them? There is nothing wrong with being childless. Wouldn't it be better not to have children than to leave them without their parents and home life for years at a time? I'm not sure. All I know is that God's perspective is not the same as ours, and he can bring great good out of our choices, no matter how painful and even wrong they might look to us at the time. Hannah gave up her son Samuel, and it was a right choice. The same can be said, it seems, for Evelyn Brand. Even as Samuel grew up to serve the Lord, so did Paul and Connie. Indeed, Paul Brand went on to become a missionary and a world-renowned surgeon who made medical history with his breakthroughs in leprosy treatment.

As painful as his mother's choices were for Paul himself to deal with, ultimately he owed much of his own strength of character and commitment to missions to the example set by his mother. When Evelyn was seventy-five and partially disabled by a fractured hip, Paul visited her in India and pleaded with her to retire. She was not impressed with his argument. Who would take her place if she left? There was nobody else to do the medical work and the itinerant preaching. Far better, she reasoned, to die in God's service than to live in retirement without ministry.

As a medical doctor and as a son Paul was distressed by his mother's decision, but he could not help admiring her unwavering commitment to God and to the people she had been called to serve. His tribute to her speaks for itself:

> And so she stayed. Eighteen years later, at the age of ninety-three, she reluctantly gave up sitting on her pony because she was falling off all too frequently. Devoted Indian villagers began bearing her on a hammock from town to town. After two more years of mission work, she finally died at the age of ninety-five. . . .
>
> One of my last and strongest visual memories of my mother is set in a village in the mountains she loved. . . . She is sitting on a low stone wall that circles the village, with people pressing in from all sides. . . . They are looking at a wrinkled old face but . . . to them, she is beautiful.[3]

Most missionary parents today do not face Evelyn's painful choice. Boarding schools and other options are available so that children are rarely separated from their parents for more than a few months at a time. But even Evelyn had options—such as going to an area where schooling for her children would have been available. Yet that initial painful choice set her on a course that allowed God to work in her life and the lives of her children, and in the process influenced millions.

Painful choices are always the hardest choices to make. We go back and forth, struggling to make up our minds, and in the end we are often uncertain whether we have made the right decision. We search the Bible for answers, but even then we are prone to find what seem to be conflicting messages from the Lord. "Anyone who loves his father or mother more than me is not worthy of me; anyone who loves his son or daughter more than me is not worthy of me," are the words of Jesus in Matthew 10:37. Evelyn Brand could have taken that verse as direction as she made her painful choice to leave her son and daughter. On the other hand, she might have looked to Scriptures in both the Old and New Testaments that admonish parents to instruct their children in the ways of the Lord on a continual basis: "Teach [God's Word] to your children, talking about them when you sit at home and when you walk along the road, when you lie down and when you get up" (Deut. 11:19); "Bring them up in the training and instruction of the Lord" (Eph. 6:4). These passages assume parents' personal involvement in their children's spiritual growth and could be used to support a decision not to separate from one's children, even for the sake of the ministry.

So, then, how do we go about making painful choices? One way is to make a checklist of questions that will probe our motives and challenge us to think of options and outcomes that we might not otherwise consider:

- What does God want? The mind of God, as we have already seen, is often difficult to discern, but do I have a strong sense that this painful choice will further the kingdom of God and his work in my life? Have I sought God in prayer over his will in this choice? Have I been listening for the prompting and guidance of the Holy Spirit?
- What are my underlying motives in this choice? This may require us to probe far beneath the surface and ask ourselves some pointed questions. Am I seeking pain in an effort to appear more spiritual to my family or friends? Am I desiring to draw attention and

sympathy? Are there any shades of a martyr complex in my choice? Am I seeking credit for suffering?

- Am I avoiding pain at all costs? Am I forfeiting eternal values to prevent the pain of the moment? This is the most common challenge we must give ourselves as we face painful choices. Am I making a wrong choice simply to avoid pain?
- How will this painful choice affect others? Will my pain be offset by the benefit it brings to others? Will this choice cause others pain? Is that pain justifiable?
- Can I legitimately reduce the pain? We should not be afraid to look for and consider alternatives that would be less painful to ourselves and others, without reducing the positive gains.
- Can I turn this pain into positive results? When alternatives do not arise, we should look for beneficial gains. Can this choice make me a better person? Am I willing to let this painful choice draw me closer to God? Will it teach me to more readily depend on others and broaden my support group? Am I now less judgmental of others who are making painful choices?
- How can I help others through my pain? Can I use my painful choice to encourage others who are enduring similar times of decision making? Our choices should always focus outward.
- Do I experience a sense of peace? This can be a false sense, of course, and we must guard against that. On the other hand, even when the choice is right we may sense very little peace. In most instances, however, a deep sense of peace is an ideal final indicator and an assurance that we have made the right choice.

The sequel to a painful choice is a healing choice. Whether we consciously choose pain or not, there are choices to be made in the healing process. I often read about people who have lost loved ones to cancer or a drunken driver or AIDS, and have, as part of their healing process, chosen to become involved in countering these adversities.

In such circumstances our choices can help or hinder the healing process. We can become reclusive, or we can keep functioning whether we feel like it or not. We can talk about our loved one and establish a memorial, or we can clench our teeth in silence. It's our choice.

The woman who is raped or the woman who is physically mutilated by a mastectomy or the woman who is devastated by her son's homosexuality all have healing choices to make. As difficult as these circumstances are, they are made tolerable through healing choices.

We are sometimes fooled into thinking that people who bemoan their problems the most are the ones with the worst problems, but studies have shown this is not true. It is often the ones who endure the most pain who recover most fully. Why? Because they have made healing choices.

Painful choices hurt. There is no getting around that fact, and we must be prepared to face those choices and grow through the pain. Painful choices are not for the moment. They are made with one eye on the future and the other eye on eternity.

> *Considered in themselves, painful things can never be loved, but considered in the light of their source—as ordained by Providence and the will of God—they are infinitely delightful.*
> *—St. Francis of Sales*
> *"Treatise on the Love of God," 1607*

Eleven

Compromising Choices

*Jochebed's decision to serve as a nursemaid for her own son who was "kidnapped" by Pharaoh's daughter was: **(a)** the only way out of a bad situation, **(b)** a sign of weakness and lack of trust in God, **(c)** a clever maneuver that saved her son, **(d)** a risky choice that pointed to potential disaster.*

Miriam's heart was pounding. She had prayed that the floating-basket trick would save her little brother from Pharaoh's rampage. But now Pharaoh's daughter and her servants had come down to the river to bathe and seemed pulled like a magnet to the basket floating in reeds. If there was any consolation in this tense drama, it was that Pharaoh himself was not the one whose bath had been disrupted by the cries of the infant. Pharaoh was a monstrous killer, so insecure about his own leadership and so fearful of the Israelites enslaved in Egypt that he had decreed that all Hebrew baby boys should be drowned in the Nile River.

I've often wondered why Jochebed, the mother of Moses, chose to hide her little one in a basket in the very river in which Pharaoh would have had him drowned. That is certainly the last place I would have chosen. But perhaps Jochebed thought the Nile would be the last place anyone would ever expect to find a Hebrew baby.

And why this particular place? If Pharaoh's daughter was coming there to bathe that day, it would not be unreasonable to assume that she had bathed there before, perhaps on

153

a regular basis. So why on earth would Jochebed take such a chance? Was she stupid? I don't think so.

As I read and reread that story in the second chapter of Exodus, I also read between the lines, and I begin to suspect that Jochebed may have left her son in the river *hoping* he would be found by the Egyptian princess. Perhaps Jochebed had observed the princess and her attendants on previous bathing excursions. If the princess found the baby, Jochebed could have reasoned, there might be a ray of hope. Even though she was Pharaoh's daughter, she was still a woman— a woman whose maternal instincts might just outweigh her loyalty to her father and to his decree.

Besides, the entire scene plays like something plotted out ahead of time. First, they barely get the basket in the water when the princess arrives on the scene. Then Miriam stands "at a distance *to see what would happen*" (Exod. 2:4, italics mine), almost as though she is expecting the princess to find her brother. And when the princess does discover him, Miriam moves right in from her stakeout position to offer a ready solution: "Shall I go and get one of the Hebrew women to nurse the baby for you?" (2:7).

It is doubtful that Miriam duped Pharaoh's daughter into believing that she was just an innocent bystander and that the Hebrew woman would be equally detached. The princess must have had more than a few suspicions about this tidy solution, but she agreed. It was either that or sentence this beautiful baby boy to death. So Jochebed was permitted to raise her own son—but not as her own son.

This was a compromise Jochebed was willing to accept, and a choice that saved Moses' life and prepared him for God's calling.

Compromising choices are not always this clear-cut, of course, and must be made discriminately. We must beware of any compromise that would damage our reputation or the reputation of the gospel. For example, as an adult Moses discontinued this particular compromise with a decision that placed him forever in the Hebrews 11 "Hall of Faith": "By faith Moses, when he had grown up, refused to be known as the son of Pharaoh's daughter. He chose to be mistreated along with the people of God rather than to enjoy the pleasures of sin for a short time. He regarded disgrace for the sake of Christ as of greater value than the treasures of Egypt, because he was looking ahead to his reward" (Heb. 11:24–26).

Many of the decisions we confront in life offer the opportunity for compromise. Like Moses, we must avoid compromising simply for pleasure or material gain. Indeed, our lives can be ruined by one such misjudged choice.

Morals, ethics, and truth in general often beg to be compromised. Unless we are cautious, we can easily slide into compromising choices before we know it. We warn young people about avoiding compromising situations, but as adults we face the same kinds of temptations in the workplace and in our social relationships.

I look back with regret on a time when I sold encyclopedias door-to-door during my summer vacations from college. The encyclopedias were high quality, and I was fully justified in pointing out to people that it was far better to spend their money on encyclopedias than on cigarettes. But I sometimes went along with company practices that were less than ethical—such as convincing people to buy the product when they really couldn't afford it or using tricks of the trade and sales gimmicks that compromised my own standards.

Another area that catches us unaware is that which relates to our faith. My spiritual roots are in a brand of fundamentalism where *compromise* was a dirty word. One of the forms it took was forbidding fellowship with any Christians who did not believe exactly the way we did. While I am no longer a member of a church that would forbid such fellowship and can now revel in ecumenical gatherings, I have not discarded my heritage altogether.

As a church historian I know how easy it is for individual Christians as well as entire denominations to slide into compromise just for the sake of keeping the peace. Historic doctrines of the faith as well as the authority of Scripture itself have been called into question in an effort to avoid offending anyone. Even as I write, two major denominations are debating issues of sexuality. Delegates are pleading for compromise and inclusion so that the younger generation and gays and lesbians will not be offended.

Women, who are often prone to be peacemakers, need to be especially wary of falling into this trap of compromising to please everyone. Yes, we must reach out in love to others, but not at the expense of our faith that is rooted in the Word of God.

Yet there are many choices in life where compromise is required, or at least preferable. In these instances we relinquish certain benefits for the sake of a greater good. For Jochebed this meant giving up her son in order to spare his life. For us it might mean something as mundane as having to forfeit one's privacy and share an apartment in order to save money for a down payment on a house.

Young couples often face compromising choices as they plan for children. Perhaps the wife's, or the husband's, graduate school studies have to be delayed or tackled at a slower rate. Families sometimes encounter compromising choices when they contemplate job transfers. Do they uproot the family or do they pass up the job promotion? These are tough choices that often demand nothing short of compromise—accepting something less than ideal for the long-term benefit of the family.

Compromising choices require creative thinking and willingness to bend, and in the end they are never ideal, never completely satisfying. But they offer alternatives to otherwise difficult or impossible situations.

I am reminded of the mother I recently read about who felt housebound with her two young children. She longed to enroll in graduate studies but could not because of time and money considerations. So she made a compromising choice—not her ideal, but an option that served her well until she was able to begin her graduate studies. She searched out library story hours for children, and while her little ones were enjoying the storytelling, she had time to browse the shelves and read books and articles in her own self-styled graduate education.

It is tempting to polarize situations: to plan for a particular ideal, and when it fails to materialize respond as though we must accept its polar opposite. When weather-bound in an airport on the way home for Thanksgiving, the natural response is to wallow in misery. But a compromising choice that falls somewhere between the enjoyment of a Thanksgiving dinner and the misery of an airport might be finding a corner in which to read a good book or spend time praying, meditating, and reflecting on life—activities that, in fact, might have more lasting, positive impact than the Thanksgiving dinner.

Compromising choices are the stuff of good relation-ships, whether among friends or coworkers or family members. If we live and work in solitude, as the medieval hermits did, we can avoid the inconvenience of compromise in our relationships. But if we are part of a community, we frequently have no other choice but to willingly submit to something that would not be our first option.

Indeed, the most often quoted household code in the New Testament, found in Ephesians 5 and 6, begins with the admonition, "Submit to one another out of reverence for Christ" (5:21). What follows is a timeless standard for both private and public relationships: in all our relational choices there must be the give and take of compromise, of submitting ourselves to one another, whether in the home or in the workplace.

Some would have us believe that marriage is a one-sided relationship, with one partner submitting and the other being submitted to—the submitter and the submittee. But in a truly good marriage the pattern is more like an evenly balanced seesaw. It goes back and forth, with compromising choices on both sides, as opposed to the kind of compromise Mark Twain poked fun of in one of his short stories. When Mrs. McWilliams insisted on installing a burglar alarm, Mr. McWilliams acquiesced in the decision, as he testifies: "I agreed to this compromise. I will explain that whenever I want a thing, and Mrs. McWilliams wants another thing, and we decide upon the thing that Mrs. McWilliams wants—as we always do—she calls that a compromise."[1]

Even as husbands and wives work out compromises, so must parents and children. After seventeen years of experience, my son and I have a highly developed pattern of give-and-take, but even with all that practice we sometimes run into snags, usually because one of us has failed to make the necessary compromise.

As a coauthor of two books, I also know the necessity of compromise in close working partnerships. From the initial organization and writing of a book to the final editing and marketing, there are knotty issues to deal with and personal styles to mesh together. All this requires compromise, but in the process the final product is invariably improved.

Failure to compromise, on the other hand, impedes progress and can negatively affect our Christian witness. Paul pleaded with Euodia and Syntyche to "agree with each other in the Lord" (Phil. 4:2). Here was a case where apparently neither party would budge, and eventually their disagreement affected the whole church.

Paul did not take sides, so presumably this was not a matter of right and wrong, but one that begged for compromise. The problem was so serious, however, that it required outside assistance. "Help these women who have contended at my side in the cause of the gospel," Paul requested straightforwardly (4:3). They needed someone to assist them in coming together in a compromise—not the "help" of people taking sides and further deepening the differences.

Sometimes we find ourselves caught in the middle of delicate situations that not only call for compromise but also demand the art of diplomacy. One little mistake could magnify the problem or ruin a friendship.

I'll never forget the time during my college days in Texas when I was summoned to the dean's office and asked to "rat" on my friend Kay. Kay was a clever prankster, but this time she had gone too far. She had raided the dresser drawer of her rival, a popular coed down the hall, and then handed over the girl's underwear to a fraternity house—sort of a reverse panty raid, I guess. I quickly learned that Kay was the culprit, and I wasn't impressed with what she had done. But when the dean called me in, knowing I had an inside track on most pranks, I was not inclined to inform on her.

This was a Christian college back in the 1960s, and discipline was tight under Dean Wiley. He offered me two choices: give him the name of the guilty person or remain silent and stay in his office, presumably until I "cracked." But as he continued to press me for the information, I suggested a compromise. I would not give him a name, but I would go to the guilty person as a friend and strongly encourage her to turn herself in, providing he could assure me that it would be in her best interest to do so. He permitted me to leave, and Kay did turn herself in—a happy ending to a compromising choice, at least for me. I don't recall what punishment Kay received.

Compromising choices usually are not ideal, but they are the best choices for less than ideal circumstances. Jochebed's choice was either give her son to Pharaoh's daughter or have him die at the hands of the Egyptians. It was a life and death matter.

Paul also chose life over death—a choice he regarded as less than ideal, but one that most effectively served the cause of the gospel. "For to me to live is Christ and to die is gain. If I am to go on living in the body, this will mean fruitful labor for me. Yet what shall I choose? I do not know! I am torn between the two: I desire to depart and be with Christ, which is better by far; but it is more necessary for you that I remain in the body" (Phil. 1:21–24).

Paul surely recognized that the ultimate choice in this instance was God's, but he was willing to make the best of what was less desirable. And so it was, in quite different circumstances, with Velma Barfield.

Velma Barfield's childhood in an impoverished area of rural North Carolina was marred by incest and abuse, and as a black female she faced discrimination at every turn. But these strikes against her had no effect on the judge and jury during Velma's trial in 1978 for the murder of her fiancé, her mother, and two other people.

Velma admitted her guilt, but she also testified that she was hooked on drugs, a condition that apparently was a factor in the murders. She was convicted on four counts of first-degree murder and sentenced to be executed.

For Velma, the only alternatives seemed to be opposite extremes: the "miracle" of having the sentence overturned and being set free, or the inevitable horrors of death row followed by execution. But Velma made a compromising choice. Determined to make the best of an awful situation, she became, in the words of Billy Graham, "the pulpit on death row."

The initial step in this decision came one night when a guard tuned his radio to the voice of an evangelist. Velma had been familiar with the gospel message as a child and young adult, but it had never pierced her conscience. Now she was in an awful mess, and she realized that message was for her. She committed her life to Christ right there in her jail cell.

For the next six years, while she waited on death row for her execution, Velma became an evangelist and minister to those around her. Her story was published, and her testimony influenced countless others. Billy Graham's wife, Ruth, became aware of Velma's situation and began corresponding with her. Ruth wrote to Velma:

> God has turned your cell on Death Row into a most unusual pulpit. There are people who will listen to what you have to say because of where you are. As long as God has a ministry for you here, He will keep you here. When I compare the dreariness, isolation, and difficulty of your cell to the glory that lies ahead of you, I could wish for your sake that God would say, "Come on Home."

Velma's "going home" wish was realized in 1984 when she became the first woman in more than two decades to be executed in the United States. But she was ready. To Ruth Graham she had written: "If I am executed on August 31, I know the Lord will give me dying grace, just as He has given me saving grace, and has given me living grace."[2]

Velma made a choice that turned her short life around and opened the gates to eternity. Faced with opposite extremes, she made the best of compromise.

My friend Margaret is right now facing a similar choice, although in entirely different circumstances. Four years ago as a result of breast cancer she had a mastectomy, and the following year she had the other breast removed just to be safe. She thought she was out of danger, but then another lump appeared under her arm. Last summer her doctors at Mayo Clinic told her that further surgery or even chemo-therapy or radiation would be of no help—that her cancer would inevitably spread to the lymph nodes and then to the vital organs and bones. Not always, though. She had a fifteen percent chance of surviving more than five years.

What a terrible sentence that was. She wasn't in prison, but to Margaret, as she and her husband walked out of Mayo Clinic that day, it seemed as bad as being sentenced to the electric chair. She was only forty-five years old, and it seemed so unfair.

Like Velma, though, Margaret has determined to make the best of this bad situation. It's not a death sentence, she insists, and there's no time for self-pity and hopelessness. Indeed, she is convinced that she is among that fifteen percent who will survive beyond the five years. And however long she has, she has vowed to live life to the fullest—enjoying her husband and three children and taking control of her own situation.

Hers is a compromising choice. While staying in close contact with her doctors, she has been reading every book and article she can find on nontraditional techniques for beating cancer. She's drinking carrot juice by the quart and is taking an assortment of vitamins. She's also exercising, and, perhaps a bit more controversial to some, she spends time visualizing her good cells attacking the diseased ones. But most of all she's trusting God, confident that she is entirely in his hands. When I spent a day at the beach with her recently, she was as beautiful and vibrant and physically fit as she was the day she walked down the aisle twenty-four years ago as my maid of honor.

Rarely are we faced with compromising choices in situations as extreme as Velma's or Margaret's or Jo-chebed's. In most instances these choices involve everyday challenges that require us to make the best of bad situations or lower our standards or expectations for what we think is best. When to compromise and when not to, however, requires discernment—discernment that is enhanced if we are prepared to question and analyze the situation at various levels.

- Do I have a compromising spirit? Am I willing to submit to others and seek compromise when there is disagreement? Am I eager to make the best of bad situations?
- Does my choice compromise my Christian principles? Does it weaken the authority of Scripture or my moral and ethical standards?
- Am I skeptical of compromise by nature, presuming that compromise is always inferior to one side or another? Does my upbringing or personality deter me from compromise?
- Does my compromising choice foster unity? Does it avert strife? Does it help heal relationships? Am I eager for opportunities to mediate conflicts?
- Does my choice offer an alternative to a bad situation when a good solution seems impossible? Does it model a truly Christian perspective?

My *Random House College Dictionary* offers positive, neutral, and negative definitions of *compromise*: as a positive it is "a settlement of differences by mutual concessions"; as a neutral it is "something intermediate between different things"; and as a negative it is "an endangering, esp. of reputation" or "to make a dishonorable or shameful concession."

These definitions illustrate the contradictory nature of compromise and the potential for harm when we make compromising choices. But there is also a danger in avoiding compromising choices, especially if we are prone, as many of us are, to see things only in extremes. These individuals, writes Patricia Gundry, "tend to come from rigid parental backgrounds. Early on, they were required to obey strict parents. They always had to determine between two choices: the right way and the wrong way." They "think in black and white" and "give themselves only two choices whenever possible."[3]

We often severely limit our options when compromising choices are not considered. Indeed, what a tragedy it might have been had Jochebed contemplated only the opposite extremes confronting baby Moses: the worst scenario of almost-certain death at Pharaoh's hands or the best (and unlikely) scenario of a normal life in a Hebrew family household. She was a woman who made a God-honoring compromising choice—a model for us today.

Mankind likes to think in terms of extreme opposites. It is given to formulating its beliefs in terms of Either-Ors, *between which it recognizes no intermediate possibilities. When forced to recognize that the extremes cannot be acted upon, it is still inclined to hold that they are all right in theory, but that when it comes to practical matters circumstances compel us to compromise.*

—*John Dewey*
Experience and Education

Twelve

Confrontational Choices

Vashti's refusal to titillate the drunken guests at her husband's royal banquet was: **(a)** *a certain and speedy road to divorce,* **(b)** *a rash defiance of her husband the king,* **(c)** *an act of moral courage in the face of unbeatable odds,* **(d)** *the first recorded feminist protest.*

V*ashti has gotten bad press* over the centuries—Vashti, the queen who is deposed and quickly relegated to obscurity in the book of Esther. Male Bible commentators seem to have little sympathy for this woman who publicly defied her husband and, in doing so, set a bad example for women throughout the country. Besides, if Vashti had prevailed in the showdown with King Xerxes, Jewish history might have been very different.

Still, in my mind Vashti was an admirable woman—at least in this instance. Born a Persian princess, she married the powerful King Xerxes who reigned over more than a hundred provinces from India to Ethiopia. But there is no hint in the biblical account that Vashti was some kind of harem feminist seeking to undermine her husband's authority or gain personal fame or power. Her action was not meant to eclipse her husband, but to maintain her proper role as a queen.

We are told that during the king's extravagant seven-day banquet when "the royal wine was abundant . . . Queen Vashti also gave a banquet for the women" (Est. 1:7, 9). But that was not enough, at least not in the eyes of her husband.

165

On the seventh day of his week-long bash, the king, now "in high spirits from wine," commanded Vashti to present herself in front of all the party goers "to display her beauty . . . for she was lovely to look at" (1:10, 11).

Her response was resolute. She refused to go. That's all we're told, and we wish we had more details. Did she seek a compromise? Did she discuss the situation with her best friend or advisor? Was she upset about her husband's extravagant drinking party? Did she realize the implications of her refusal? Was she incensed by her husband's outrageous demand? We simply do not know.

We do know, however, that holding true to her Eastern culture and upbringing she would have no part of this charade. She could never show off her body in this way to a man other than her husband. Xerxes himself must have been aware of the total inappropriateness of his request— unless he is to be excused on the grounds of drunkenness. Whatever the consequences, though, Queen Vashti dared to defy the king.

I ask myself what I would have done in a situation like that. I tend to be cautious about decision making when my future security is on the line. Would I have been tempted to let my standards slip just this one time to avoid the confrontation? Apparently Vashti's courage and inner resources served her well on this occasion.

"Her self-respect and her high character meant more to her than her husband's vast realm," writes Herbert Lockyer. "Rather than cater to the vanity and sensuality of the drunkards, she courageously sacrificed a kingdom." The commentator then goes on to suggest that "The only true ruler in that drunken court was the woman who refused to exhibit herself, even at the king's command."[1]

King Xerxes must have been an insecure man. His extravagant display of wealth ought to give us a clue to that, but even more so, his reaction to Vashti's refusal. It is understandable that he would be furious with her, especially considering his condition and surroundings. But after he sobered up, we would expect him to try to put the embarrassing incident behind him. Not this Persian autocrat. Upon the advice of his "wise men" it was decreed that Queen Vashti was "never again to enter the presence of King Xerxes" and that the king would "give her royal position to someone else who [was] better than she" (Est. 1:19).

This decree was written "in the laws of the Medes and the Persians," which meant it could never—absolutely never—be repealed. The rationale behind this royal edict was to offset the "feminist" protest of the queen: "For this deed of the queen will be made known to all women, causing them to look with contempt on their husbands" (1:17 NRSV) With the decree in force, the king and his advisors reasoned, "all the women will respect their husbands, from the least to the greatest" (1:20).

Vashti's confrontational choice resulted in her downfall. She was deposed, and Esther was eventually chosen to fill her place. Confrontational choices do not always end like this, but they do involve risks. A woman who confronts her domineering boss or her abusive husband risks losing her job or her marriage, but she also sets the stage for rectifying an intolerable situation. Confrontation with conviction is a powerful tool, and while there may be loss—a job or friends or prestige—there is still the satisfaction in having done what was right.

Jesus chose this path when he drove the profiteers out of the temple. He could have passed right by these money changers bartering for birds in the temple. After all, everyone else accepted their presence, including the chief priests and teachers of the law. Instead, Jesus chose to confront them, and in doing so he risked his very life: "The chief priests and the teachers of the law heard this and began looking for a way to kill him" (Mark 11:18). There are times for confrontation with conviction, as Jesus modeled throughout his perfect life.

When do we choose to confront and when do we walk on by? Recently I faced that very question. I had taken my car to be repaired. As I was explaining the problem to the owner of this mom-and-pop auto shop, he suddenly switched the conversation to his own problems with vandalism. Then, without warning, he blurted out several racist slurs.

Rather than confront him about this, I finished my business and got on my bike and headed home, leaving my car with this racist mechanic whose work I trusted and whose prices were much more reasonable than the dealership where I had purchased the car. But all the way home I felt guilty. How would Mrs. Hall, my next-door neighbor, or Claretha and Jack, two houses down, feel about me if they knew I had just stood there while someone maligned their race?

Had I failed to stand up for my convictions? If these racist slurs had come from a friend or an acquaintance at church, I wouldn't have let them pass. In the case of my auto mechanic, however, it seemed the best thing to do. So why do I still feel so guilty?

Confrontational choices require discernment and timing, and we do well to heed the writer of Ecclesiastes who reminds us that there is "a time to tear down and a time to build" and "a time for war and a time for peace" (Eccl. 3:3, 8). While not speaking directly to the issue of confrontational choices, this passage does emphasize the legitimate place of conflict in life. Traditionally, however, women are trained to avoid confrontation.

Many young girls, especially in my generation, grew up observing their mothers take the peacemaker role, and when they themselves became confrontational on the playground or in the classroom they were told that such behavior was not appropriate for girls. Girls played dolls with make-believe family arrangements, while boys played "army" or "cowboys and Indians." So should we be surprised that we tend to focus on building others up and keeping the peace?

Certainly there is much to be said for keeping the peace, and some disagreeable situations are better left unaddressed. I am learning that more and more every day with my teenage son. Some issues do call for confrontation, but when I back away and allow the less pressing issues to dissipate, I can almost always say I have made the right choice.

This principle also holds when dealing with adults. Should a woman confront her daughter-in-law about her messy house and ill-behaved children? Should she confront her sister about wearing too much make-up? Should we confront a friend about bad breath? Should we confront a coworker about her extended coffee breaks?

When Paul admonished Christians to speak "the truth in love," he seemed to be speaking about a larger Truth (Eph. 4:15). When it comes to everyday issues, however, this same principle ought to apply to any confrontational choices we make. And there are times, perhaps in the particular examples above, when another principle may be even more applicable: MYOB (mind your own business!), that favored acronym of Ann Landers.

Yet there is often a fine line between MYOB and speaking the truth in love. If the ill-behaved grandchildren are ruining your flower gardens, or if the coworker's coffee-break cigarette smoke is filtering into your office space, the latter principle ought to apply.

And when applying the principle, we must remember to employ the right techniques: focusing on wrong actions and issues, rather than on the persons themselves, and avoiding acrimony and sarcasm. We should also avoid the temptation to recruit support and gang up on the offending individual—except when appropriate as a last resort.

I used this gang-up game plan years ago when I was in graduate school at a large church-related university, and it backfired on me. At the time I was an assistant dorm resident director, and the offending individual was my boss, the dean of women, who was making a behind-the-scenes effort to have Campus Crusade for Christ banned from campus. Since Roman Catholic and other denominational religious groups were permitted to freely hold meetings on campus, I saw this as patently unfair and was determined to act. Instead of confronting her privately, I brought the issue up in the monthly dorm directors' meeting, where I knew I would have wide support. My method of confrontation was successful. The dean backed down. But I had outmaneuvered her publicly, and in the months that followed she made me pay dearly by undermining my relationship with my dorm residents until I ended up quitting my position.

I have often questioned the appropriateness of that confrontational choice. Had I approached the dean privately, would I have prevented the hurt feelings and anger? Without the public pressure would she have backed down? Perhaps the outcome was worth the offense to her and my own ensuing problems. The cause was just, and it may have merited public confrontation. Perhaps it even kept her from trying the same initiative again after I had graduated.

In hindsight we go back and forth, wondering if we made the right choice. This is particularly common with women, who sometimes face negative consequences for being confrontational. Such conduct is not feminine, we are told. When we reflect on history, though, it is the strong, confrontational women who stand out—women who rose up in protest, even though they knew they would be targeted as "stepping out of line."

Katherine Zell is one such woman. She was a sixteenth-century Protestant Reformer. That may surprise many people, for according to the history books the Reformers were men—Martin Luther, John Calvin, Ulrich Zwingli, John Knox, and others. But if we dig a little deeper we find women, like Katherine Zell, who also rose up to defend their convictions, though often on different issues and with a different style.

Katherine's first confrontation related to her gender. She was married to Matthew Zell, a Catholic priest turned Reformer, and together they had an effective ministry in Strasbourg. Katherine was so vital to the ministry that when Matthew died it was wrongly presumed by some that she wished to take over his pulpit. She did not, but she felt compelled to stand up at his funeral and defend her femininity, so to speak.

Later on, she once again had to defend herself, this time against angry charges that she was disturbing the peace. The charges were true, at least in the sense that she was disturbing the *peace of mind* of certain male clergy. She headed a massive refugee program, edited a hymnal, wrote tracts, and made pastoral visits—all activities deemed improper for a woman.

But the issue that drew my attention to her more than any other was her confrontation with the Reformers over religious tolerance. It was not uncommon during her day for professing Christians to execute other professing Christians on the grounds of heresy. This even happened in Geneva while John Calvin, the man who laid the groundwork for my own religious tradition, wielded control in that city.

The heretic in this case was Michael Servetus, and for his non-Trinitarian beliefs he was burned at the stake. He deserved what he got, the argument went, because he had challenged the orthodoxy of the Reformers. So did the Anabaptists, the spiritual ancestors of the Mennonites, who

denied the validity of infant baptism, emphasized discipleship, and defended pacifism—crimes that merited death by
drowning and other forms of persecution.

Vowing to make a difference, Katherine lashed out at
this injustice, risking her own reputation. "Why do you rail
at Schwenckfeld?" she demanded of a Lutheran preacher.
"You talk as if you would have him burned like the poor
Servetus at Geneva. . . . You behave as if you had been
brought up by savages in a jungle. The Anabaptists are
pursued as by a hunter with dogs chasing wild boars. Yet the
Anabaptists accept Christ in all the essentials as we do."[2]

Katherine was not the only woman to protest the
violence connected with religious intolerance during the
Reformation. Renee of Ferrara, a French woman who
married into the Italian royal family, also took a strong stand
and was willing to make confrontational choices. She wrote
an angry letter to John Calvin, her mentor, condemning the
carnage carried out against Roman Catholics: "Monsieur
Calvin, I am distressed that you do not know how the half in
this realm behave. They even exhort the simple to kill and
strangle. This is not the rule of Christ. I say this out of the
great affection which I hold for the Reformed religion."[3]

Renee, like Katherine, was seen as overstepping the
bounds of femininity when she confronted her male
contemporaries. This has been true throughout history.
Indeed, it is interesting to discover how many of the women
who challenged the establishment were charged with being
"an Eve." Argula von Stauffer, who confronted the Roman
Catholic establishment in Bavaria, was described as "an
insolent daughter of Eve, a heretical bitch and confounded
rogue."[4] A century later in Colonial New England, Anne
Hutchinson, who confronted the Puritan establishment, was
accused of snaring the men into her "heresy" . . . "as by an
Eve."[5]

Even today women who make confrontational choices

run the risk of being viewed as "Eves." In fact, it has become fashionable for some biblical scholars and writers to argue that Eve's sin in the garden was role reversal—that she stepped out of line as a woman and in doing so abdicated her femininity. Elisabeth Elliot is one of the proponents of this unusual interpretation of Genesis 3: "Eve, in her refusal to accept the will of God, refused her femininity. Adam, in his capitulation to her suggestion, abdicated his masculine responsibility for her."[6]

The Bible leaves no doubt that Adam and Eve sinned, but the claim that Adam's sin was "capitulation to her suggestion" implies not only that there is sin involved in a man capitulating to a woman but that somehow the original sin might have been less serious had it been Adam who initiated the idea of eating the forbidden fruit. According to this interpretation of Scripture strong women today are "Eves," even as their confrontational forebears have been described.

This kind of intimidation is not new. From time immemorial men (and women) have sought to stifle the voices of women, particularly if they challenge the prevailing male viewpoint. What a tragedy. We need prophets, both male and female, to speak out and confront and step on toes if necessary. The only demand we make is that they speak the truth.

One contemporary women who has modeled the qualities necessary for confrontational choices is Sandra McGee Tanner, the most respected and powerful voice in Christian circles today on issues related to Mormonism. She is a prophet of sorts in this day and age when Mormonism is growing rapidly and seeking to enter the mainstream of Christianity.

Sandra McGee was raised a faithful Mormon and holds the distinction of being a great-great-granddaughter of Brigham Young. But as a young adult she began to struggle with unresolved issues. "When I started college," she recalls, "I enrolled in the Mormon Institute of Religion class. I started asking questions in class, trying to find answers to my doubts. But one day my teacher took me aside and told me to stop asking questions."[7] Sandra was too confrontational. She was challenging male authority.

Sandra was not the first confrontational woman in her family. Even before she began challenging church teachings, her grandmother had been questioning the authority of the church, and it was through her grandmother that Sandra met Jerald Tanner, who was already convinced that Mormonism was false. Sandra and Jerald married in 1959, and four months later Sandra committed her life to Christ. In 1960 the Tanners had their names removed from the rolls of the Mormon church, setting the stage for their lifelong ministry of exposing the fallacies of Mormonism.

The focus of their ministry has been research, digging into the history and doctrine of Mormonism and publishing their findings. Their first major joint publication, *The Case Against Mormonism*, was described by an evangelical leader as "the definitive, fully-documented, utterly-devastating case against the divine authority and truthfulness of the foundational documents upon which the Mormon religion is based."[8]

In 1985 the *Salt Lake Tribune* printed a feature story on the Tanners that sums up their ministry from a secular perspective: "This husband and wife team may be two of the most well-informed self-taught scholars on the subject of Mormonism in the world."[9]

Unlike Jerald, who is quiet and shuns public speaking, Sandra is eager to confront Mormons in public debate and to speak out in large assemblies. Her style is compelling as she builds her case from reams of documents and logically works through the evidence, arguing her points with clarity, humor—and sometimes tears. Sandra is known for her humor, but I have watched her in a public forum reading letters of heartbreak from Mormons and ex-Mormons, and I have seen her choke back the tears and pause momentarily until she was able to continue.

In some instances the Tanners have been charged with going too easy on the Mormons. When Mormons were accused of knowingly worshiping Lucifer, the Tanners demanded evidence and warned Christians to avoid such sensationalism. Indeed, Sandra is confrontational not only with Mormons but also with those who would wrongly accuse them—and even with her husband when she has felt that he was on the wrong course.

When a document known as the "Salamander Letter" surfaced some years ago showing how deeply Joseph Smith was involved in the occult, Sandra wrote an article arguing for its authenticity, while Jerald took the opposite perspective. Sandra's view was accepted by the Mormon church itself, which found itself doubly embarrassed when Jerald's claims that it was fraudulent were later proven correct.

Some might suggest that a wife should not publicly disagree with her husband, but Sandra and Jerald live out a true partnership, and their credibility is enhanced by their independent thinking. This is not an instance of role reversal; rather, it is role *modeling*.

Sandra's style of confrontation also is a model for all of us. Considering her awareness of the deceptive nature of Mormonism, it might be natural for her to be caustic and bitter, but Sandra assiduously avoids any tendencies in that direction. "We don't feel any hatred toward Mormons or toward their church," she insists. "We have tried to stay away from derogatory words or hostile terminology that may be offensive or belittling. Certainly our literature is meant to be hard-hitting in attacking the claims of Joseph Smith, but we've tried not to use loaded words. A few slip in now and then, but we have tried to avoid that."[10]

The confrontational choices Sandra Tanner has made over the past thirty years ought to challenge us to be willing to take a strong stand when the cause is right and just, but in some ways, because of her particular situation, her choices might seem too easy. After all, there is little debate in evangelical circles regarding the unorthodox nature of Mormonism. But what about issues where there is much debate and where the potential for bitter wrangling among believers is greater?

Paul warns that "it is good not to . . . do anything that makes your brother or sister stumble" (Rom. 14:21 NRSV), and he pleads with believers to "make every effort to keep the unity of the Spirit through the bond of peace" (Eph. 4:3). Yet Paul himself demonstrated time and again that there were issues that did merit confrontation.

So we must carefully balance the merit of the cause with the potential for disunity, while at the same time seeking alternative outlets for our confrontational choices. Perhaps the issue is the desire to permit women to serve on the deacon board of the church. If bringing the matter up at the annual business meeting promises to be divisive, a better alternative might be to focus on the issue first as a series of lessons in an adult Sunday school class.

As women, however, we must be wary of the tendency to avoid confrontation at all costs. Sometimes it is only through confrontation that progress is made. I am reminded of the origins of the Women's Missionary Movement in the late nineteenth century, a movement born of confrontation. Prior to that time women were not permitted to serve as missionaries in their own right. Any woman who wanted to go to the mission field had to be married, which meant that many single women were denied their calling. Through confrontation, however, the rules were slowly changed, and for the past century single women have made an invaluable contribution to the cause of world missions.

When making confrontational choices, we must evaluate our motives and ask ourselves penetrating questions:

- Am I choosing confrontation solely for a self-serving cause or is my agenda one that will open doors of opportunity and enrichment for others?
- Is my cause biblically sound? Are there scriptural precedents or guidelines that can aid in my struggle? How would Jesus see this issue if he were walking the earth today? Can I in good conscience pray for success in my efforts?
- How can I avoid creating dissension? Are there alternative platforms? Is the timing right?
- Where can I go for support? Can I develop a network with other women? Are there men who are willing to stake their reputations on this cause?
- How will this issue affect me and my family personally? Is it worth the cost in terms of stress and pain and potential loss of friends, job, or business contacts?

But even as we challenge our motives in stepping out and making confrontational choices, we must also examine ourselves when we fail to take the confrontational route. Are we afraid to trust God to carry us through difficult times and pave the way for positive results? It is much easier to sit back in silence and passively accept the status quo, and we are all tempted to do so. Confrontational choices are hard choices, but in many cases they are right choices.

One of the saddest days in life is the day we allow the herd-fear
to conquer the highest judgments and instincts of the soul.
—E. Stanley Jones
Victorious Living, *1936*

Thirteen

Compassionate Choices

Dorcas made compassionate choices because: **(a)** *all women in the Bible were compassionate,* **(b)** *she was a professional widow—or deaconess—whose job description was compassion,* **(c)** *she had a genuine love for other people,* **(d)** *she was a true follower of Jesus.*

I could never really identify with Dorcas. As long as I can remember, she seemed the grandmotherly sort who never made it out of the 1950s. I envisioned her in a print apron and clunky shoes sewing up little garments for orphans and rolling bandages for mission hospitals. She was the person-ification of the good woman who never loses her temper when the dog messes on the floor and who passes out homemade cookies to all the kids on the block—and never, never gossips.

But perhaps that is the wrong picture of Dorcas. (Actually "Dorcas" was just the Greek translation; her Hebrew name was Tabitha.) Tabitha holds the unique distinction of being the only person in the Bible described as "always doing good" (Acts 9:36, literally, *full of good works*). She was also the only person raised from the dead by the apostle Peter, at least the only one recorded in the Bible. From the description of that event it is obvious that Tabitha was deeply loved, for the Bible underscores the grief of all who had come to mourn her death. She would be sorely missed and so would her good deeds.

Tabitha the seamstress. That's the way we tend to

visualize her, sitting at her loom or bending over her needle—perhaps because the Scripture says that "all the widows stood around [Peter], crying and showing him the robes and other clothing . . . [she] had made while she was still with them" (9:39). But I suspect that the clothing was only significant because it was a visible act of charity. Tabitha's most compassionate deeds were ones that could not be displayed: cradling a dying child in her arms, listening to the tearful story of a young woman whose husband has been unfaithful, or swabbing the bedsores of an invalid.

Tabitha is described as a *disciple*, thereby dispelling any notion that all the disciples were men. She may have been one of the widows mentioned in the New Testament who devoted their lives to full-time ministry, perhaps living in a communal setting. But whatever her situation, she was one in a long line of women, from the early centuries to the present, who have devoted their lives to the church. Like my friend Pam, a modern Tabitha.

With her short hair and hoop earrings Pam doesn't look like a hospital chaplain—at least not to a mind given to stereotypes. Yet Pam devotes her life to heartbroken families. She cries with them and prays with them, and they never question her deep sincerity and love as they cling to her in their grief.

I like Tabitha. In a world where the primary focus is on self-fulfillment, she serves as a model of compassion and care-giving. In fact, she seems to embody the dictionary definition:

> *Compassion*: a feeling of deep sympathy and sorrow for another's suffering or misfortune, accompanied by a desire to alleviate the pain or remove its cause.

Compassionate choices often mean setting our own agenda aside, being less concerned about promotions or salary raises and more concerned with ministering to those in need. I have another friend who forgoes prestige and financial gain in order to be a foster parent to handicapped children. She is sacrificing her own personal goals, at least for the present, for the satisfaction of knowing that hurting little ones have been helped.

God is the supreme demonstration of compassion, especially as we think of God incarnate in Jesus Christ. In describing the compassion of God, the prophet Isaiah writes: "Can a mother forget the baby at her breast and have no compassion on the child she has borne? Though she may forget, I will not forget you!" (Isa. 49:15). The psalmist offers the same perspective: "As a father has compassion on his children, so the LORD has compassion on those who fear him" (Ps. 103:13).

This association of compassion with parenting—whether God or human parents—is significant. Parental compassion is a natural, God-given impulse, one that hardly requires a choice. When our inclinations do not prompt deep feelings of compassion for our own children, something is wrong with us. But compassion for those who are not our own is compassion that usually falls into the category of choice, especially in this era when the concept of the nuclear family has almost become a god to some evangelicals. Unfortunately, this focus on the family has caused some to be less compassionate toward those outside the family.

This was not true in the past. Two women in particular come to mind: Sarah Doremus and Catherine Booth. Both had large families and were not lacking in compassion for their own children. Yet their care-giving extended far beyond the confines of their immediate families.

Sarah had nine children of her own and still could have lived a life of relative leisure since her husband was an affluent businessman. Instead she chose to devote much of her life to deeds of compassion. Using her organizational skills and the sacrificial help of others, she established ministries to prisoners, homeless families, orphans, and the

elderly and in 1861 organized the Women's Union Missionary Society. Much of the financial support for these projects
came from her own household budget, and when that
allotment was spent she went into her closet and selected
items to sell for the benefit of the poor. High fashion was no
longer important to her—and hardly an asset as she walked
the alleys of the tenement districts of New York City.

At about the same time, across the Atlantic, Catherine
Booth was ministering to the poor in the slums of London.
She was married to William Booth, a pawnbroker turned
preacher who was nearly as poor as the down-and-outers in
his tiny congregations. Together they founded the Salvation
Army.

Catherine's compassion radiated in many directions, but
she was particularly distressed by the plight of prostitutes.
With daughters of her own it might have seemed natural for
Catherine to shun this type of work, but she was willing to
take whatever risks there were to bring these young women
into the kingdom of God. It is worth noting that as the
Booth daughters grew to adulthood they followed their
mother and father into the ministry of the Salvation Army
and became leaders in their own right.

Why did these women choose compassion for others—
never an easy choice, and doubly difficult in their circumstances? Women without the modern conveniences we take
for granted, women with families three and four times the
size of our average families, women who feared crime and
negative influences as much as we do today.

"But isn't our family to be our top priority?" some will
ask. Perhaps we should ask instead, "What is the family?" or
"Is the 'traditional' family biblical?" This question was the
title of an article in *Christianity Today*, in which writer
Rodney Clapp argued that "for the Christian, church is First
Family. The biological family, though still valuable and
esteemed, is Second Family."[1] We are to reach out to our

extended family—the church—and serve those who are hurting, even as we would serve those in our biological families.

Despite this "me generation" focus on ourselves and our own immediate families, there are modern women who make compassionate choices. One is Rose Sims, an ordained Methodist minister who specializes in opening closed churches. Her secret of success is taking Paul's admonition to the Colossians very seriously: "As God's chosen people, holy and dearly loved, clothe yourselves with *compassion*, kindness, humility, gentleness and patience" (Col. 3:12).

One of the closed churches Rose Sims opened was the United Methodist Church of Trilby, Florida. She and her husband, Jim, retired to that rural community in 1984, where they found "a run-down, turn-of-the-century-vintage sanctuary with a rusty roof and a ramshackle lean-to." There were only a few active members, but "from the minute I walked in," recalls Rose, "I saw it filled with people."

For Rose and Jim the first step in revitalizing the church was initiating a plan to meet the physical needs of the people. Realizing that poverty was a reality for many of the people in the area, Rose became convinced that the church must be more than a place to meet for worship on Sunday. After recruiting help to renovate the building, she opened a used clothing distribution center and, with the assistance of county health workers, began a free clinic offering prenatal care to expectant mothers and vaccinations to preschool children.

Soon the congregation was sponsoring a Scout troop, senior citizens activities, Alcoholics Anonymous, and a singles group that distributed food to needy families. The church had become a community center and the membership was growing.

For those who worried that the church might attract too many people who did not subscribe to Christian principles,

Rose had a ready answer: "God doesn't clean His fish before He catches them." And God catches fish through people with compassion. "Love them, help them, let them know there is salvation in Jesus Christ," is Rose's self-described method, which also includes "hugging nearly everyone" who attends her church. By 1989, five years after she had been called to the Trilby church, the membership exceeded two hundred, "mostly on professions of faith."

Rose's extraordinary ministry has not gone unnoticed. She won the Circuit Rider Award for church growth, and Florida newspapers have covered her work at Trilby in feature items. But Rose's story began long before Trilby. She is a seasoned specialist in compassionate choices.

Half a century ago Rose and her first husband began their work as partners opening dead churches—first as Baptists and then as Methodists. Along the way, as they moved from one small community to another in the Midwest, Rose gave birth to three children, adopted two more, raised several foster children, and earned her doctorate in educational psychology. She dreamed of settling into college teaching, with her husband taking the major load of church responsibilities, but that dream was short-lived.

Rose's husband died in 1971, leaving her alone with his request that she devote her time to New Hope, a dead country church. With the help of fourteen families who were converted through her evangelistic outreach, Rose brought that dead church to life, living up to its name, New Hope.

When Rose subsequently met and married Jim Sims, a retired Air Force officer, it was their intention to take life easy in Florida, "to golf, sail and enjoy retirement." But God had other plans, and Rose answered his call, making just one more compassionate choice.[2]

Rose and Jim seem to thrive on their compassionate outreach to others. Rose tells how she and Jim were sitting in the Trilby church one evening when he remarked, "Haven't we had fun doing this? Haven't we been *blessed?!*"

But compassionate choices can carry negative side effects. For some, the incessant giving of self can lead to burnout—or worse. There is also the potential for becoming so involved in the needs of others that one's family is neglected. At the time of her daughter's wedding, Catherine Booth wrote of this struggle that plagued her:

> Mothers will understand . . . a side of life to which my child is yet a stranger. Having experienced the weight of public work for twenty-six years, also the weight of a large family continually hanging on my heart, having striven very hard to fulfill the obligation on both sides, and having realized what a very hard struggle it has been, the mother's heart in me has shrunk in some measure from offering her up to the same kind of warfare. . . . The consecration which I made on the morning of her birth, and consummated on the day that I gave her first to public work, I have finished this morning in laying her again on this altar.[3]

From those words it may sound as though Catherine Booth had given too much. Yet measured in terms of those she helped, she could never have given too much. And, as is so often true, her compassion multiplied itself. Many of those young women, "reclaimed" in her extended family, went out to reclaim others and became full-time workers for the Salvation Army.

Compassion not only multiplies as it extends outward, but also comes back to us in increased proportions, though only if we are allowing it to flow into us. It is possible to become so arrogant that we think we can keep giving without receiving. But the most energizing strategy we can develop is to allow ourselves to be served by others, and to allow ourselves to be refreshed by focusing on the successes and forgetting the failures. This is particularly important in ministries of compassion where the failures often far outnumber the successes.

Sometimes, when life becomes overwhelming, we need to pour out our heart to a trusted friend or counselor or support group. Gone are the days when such a step was considered a sign of weakness or a personality defect. It is a mistake, however, to imagine that turmoil in our own lives prevents us from ministering to others. Indeed, our best therapy is sometimes our involvement in other people's problems.

Some years ago while I was going through a distressing time in my own life, I was suddenly thrust into a position of caring for someone whose situation was far worse than my own. My friend Joan and her husband had taken an early retirement in order to serve a two-year medical mission term in Kenya. When Joan asked me to be a "daughter" to her elderly mother, Clara, little did I know that this commitment would soon involve me in an intense care-giving relationship. In fact, Joan and her husband were still enroute to Kenya when her mother had to be admitted to the hospital for what turned out to be inoperable cancer.

For the next several weeks I visited Clara at the hospital every day. I looked forward to those visits because they made me feel needed, and they made me realize that my problems were manageable in comparison to her physical problems that were beyond her control. Our friendship grew as we ministered to each other.

Indeed, as I look back now four years later, I know that it was Clara more than anyone else who brought me through that tough time. I was supposed to be the compassionate care-giver, the "daughter" who would be close by to help her. But as so often happens, it was not one-sided.

I was at the hospital with Clara the night before she died. We talked about the beautiful fall colors she was missing that year for the first time, and our conversation drifted naturally to heaven, a place where Michigan's glorious autumn would pale in comparison. That night I felt closer to God and to heaven than ever before, and whenever that memory resurfaces I am reminded that healing comes through serving others.

For people like Catherine Booth and Sarah Doremus and Ruth Sims compassion is a full-time ministry. For most of us, however, compassionate choices are ones we make with only a part-time commitment in mind. As a writer and teacher, the bulk of my time is devoted to creative or academic pursuits. But if I am not making compassionate choices, if I am not taking the time to give selflessly to others, something is missing from my life and I am less than a whole person.

Sometimes my compassionate choices are connected with my work: when I go out of my way to help a hurting student, perhaps someone who is not even in one of my classes. Sometimes my compassionate choices are connected with people in my neighborhood or church. But more often I fail to make a compassionate choice because I am *too busy*.

Busyness is not just an excuse. I *am* busy—with writing projects, speaking engagements, seminary classes, and all the work and activities that come with being a homemaker and mother. But much of my busyness is by choice, and here is where the issue of making compassionate choices rises up to challenge me. Why do I agree to write another article instead of spending that time reaching out to someone in need? Is it because I desire the prestige I receive from that wider recognition? Bathing an incontinent, bedridden, disabled adult offers no prestige or recognition. Am I willing to forego this world's honors?

I am often reminded of Dr. Henri Nouwen, the highly respected Catholic priest who left his prestigious position at Harvard University to go to Daybreak, a community for handicapped individuals in Toronto. There, one of his responsibilities was to care for Adam, a profoundly retarded young adult, described by many as a "vegetable." But it was through his care for Adam that Nouwen developed an inner peace that was not to be found at Harvard: "The longer I stayed with Adam the more clearly I saw him as my gentle teacher, teaching me what no book, school or professor could ever teach me."[4]

It is tempting to think of compassionate choices as optional—the choices we will fit into our lives when we retire or the obligations we get out of the way with a yearly Christmas caroling party at the local nursing home. But Jesus thought otherwise. Serving others, he taught, is comparable to rendering service to Christ himself and must be a part of the Christian life. And the consequences of not performing such service are serious:

> Then he will say to those on his left, "Depart from me, you who are cursed, into the eternal fire prepared for the devil and his angels. For I was hungry and you gave me nothing to eat, I was thirsty and you gave me nothing to drink, I was a stranger and you did not invite me in, I needed clothes and you did not clothe me, I was sick and in prison and you did not look after me."
>
> They also will answer, "Lord, when did we see you hungry or thirsty or a stranger or needing clothes or sick or in prison, and did not help you?"
>
> He will reply, "I tell you the truth, whatever you did not do for one of the least of these, you did not do for me." (Matt. 25:41–45)

Some of my most fulfilling and cherished compassionate choices have arisen spontaneously, but it is also important that our service to others be premeditated and habitual. Take time to plan for it. Otherwise the rat race of modern life will push aside this essential "nonessential" until a time when "we are no longer busy"—which never arrives.

There are many options for compassionate lay ministry, including Christian and non-Christian organizations in our own communities. But we can also develop a ministry that effectively uses our own musical, artistic, or athletic talents. One avenue that should not be overlooked is ministry to care-givers themselves: perhaps relieving a woman of her day-in and day-out care for an elderly parent who suffers from Alzheimer's disease.

Compassion is more than simply doing. Compassion is an attitude. It is service given with love, motivated by our love for God. Knowing full well that we too often serve others in a less than gracious manner, Peter reminded believers to "offer hospitality to one another without grumbling" (1 Pet. 4:9). But an uncompassionate attitude is no excuse. Better to have grumbling compassion than no compassion at all, and there is always the chance—through God's grace—that the very act of service will change our perspective.

Am I a woman of compassionate choices? Are you? Test yourself.

- Do I have a compassionate heart? Is the ministry of compassion a vital part of my Christian life? Do I see it as requisite for true Christian faith?
- How long has it been since I have voluntarily reached out in compassion to someone outside my own family? Do I make compassion a regular part of my schedule?
- Do I volunteer my services and offer compassion primarily for the praise of others? Do I have a grumbling spirit or betray a martyr complex?
- Are my compassionate choices fulfilling ones? Do I look forward to ministering to others and relish the memories of past experiences?
- Do I experience personal growth through my ministry of compassion? Am I effectively using my talents and gifts? Am I discovering qualities and gifts I didn't realize I had?
- Do I care for my own needs so I avoid burnout? Do I

allow people to minister to me even as I am offering compassion to them?

Above all, compassion must become a habit. May it be said of us, as it was of Tabitha, "She was always doing good."

Compassion is not just an exhibition of pity; it is a virtue in the strict sense of being a habit. Compassion is suffering: constant willingness to share in the suffering of others.
                                        —Hubert Van Zeller
                                        Approach to Calvary

Fourteen

Consequences of Choice

The year was 1875—a year that doesn't stand out in history. No major wars or political upheavals marked its appearance. America was in the midst of the "Gilded Age," as Mark Twain dubbed it, an age of crass materialism, financial scandals, and national self-interest. Across the Atlantic our British cousins were in the midst of the Victorian Age, an era known for prosperity and overseas expansion, named for the moralistic and straight-laced Queen Victoria. Yet it was a significant year—a year that launched the ministries of two women, one from Scotland and the other from America: Mary Slessor and Mary Baker Eddy.

One was an eminent pioneer missionary in Calabar, West Africa (present-day Nigeria); the other founded Christian Science, a religious cult. Two Marys—so very different, and yet with much in common. Both had a powerful impact on the religious life and the world of their day. Historian Margery Perham wrote that Mary Slessor "can justly be described as one of the greatest women of her generation," while humorist Mark Twain described Mary Baker Eddy as "the most daring and masculine and masterful woman that has appeared on earth in centuries."

These two women, both named for the Virgin Mary, are fascinating case studies as we contemplate the issue of multiple choices. Indeed, the marked contrast between their lives profoundly illustrates the contrast between right and wrong choices. Although these women went to their graves long ago, the consequences of their choices live on today.

191

The ongoing influence of their decisions ought to sober us as we reflect on the way our choices not only affect the course of our lives, but the lives of others as well.

Although Mary Baker Eddy was more than twenty years older than Mary Slessor, they began their successful public ministries at approximately the same time. In 1875 Mary Baker Eddy established the Christian Scientist Association, first published *Science and Health*, and withdrew her membership from the Congregational church. In that same year, Mary Slessor applied and was accepted as a missionary to Africa.

When we look at the lives of these two women, we are tempted to agree with Jean-Paul Sartre and others who would suggest that we are the sum total of our choices. Social scientists often argue that we are products of our environment, including our family heritage. While it is true that our surroundings may influence the choices we make, in the end it is not so much whether we have been victimized by a bad environment or a dysfunctional family. Rather, it is whether the process of making choices has brought us into conformity with God's will, as in the case of Mary Slessor—or drawn us away from God's will, as in the case of Mary Baker Eddy.

As we reflect on the lives of these two women, we see how they responded to the kinds of choices we have dealt with in the preceding chapters. It would be incorrect to view Mary Slessor as a model of perfection who always made right choices, and Mary Baker Eddy as just the opposite, but they are clearly a study in contrasts when it comes to the issue of choices.

Mary Slessor was one of seven children born into a poor family in the slums of Aberdeen, Scotland, in 1848. Her father was an alcoholic who "drank" the money he earned, so to support her family, Mary began working in the textile mills at the age of ten. When her father was drunk he was mean and abusive. Many times Mary Slessor, a barefoot, malnourished child, bore the brunt of his beatings after his Saturday night binges. His untimely death surely must have come as a relief both to his children and to Mary's mother, a godly woman whose strong Scottish Presbyterian influence offered Mary a heritage to build upon.

Mary Baker Eddy also had a heritage of Scottish Calvinism, but unlike Mary Slessor, she was born into relative prosperity. In addition to his farming, her father, Mark Baker, served as a justice of the peace and a chaplain of the New Hampshire militia. He was a staunch Calvinist who relished doctrinal debates, while her mother, Abigail, was a kindly woman whose religious faith took a more mellow turn. She acquiesced to her husband's demands and doted on her children, particularly Mary, her youngest, who was a sickly child subject to frequent fainting spells and convulsions and was treated as a helpless invalid.

Both Marys endured difficulties during childhood. But Mary Slessor made choices that molded her into a woman of independence and self-assurance, determined to fulfill her commitment to God's call even if it meant being a social outcast. Her life in the interior of Africa was lonely and filled with hardships, yet late in life she was able to say that she was "a witness to the perfect joy and satisfaction of a single life."

In contrast, Mary Baker Eddy made choices that kept her psychologically and physically dependent on others and often dragged them down with her during her bouts of depression and debilitating illnesses. She thrived on adulation, and seemed to be happy only when her cult followers were mesmerized by a larger-than-life image of her. Stories of her piety and miracles abounded, but her personal life was filled with problems and turmoil.

SPIRITUAL CHOICES

Mary Slessor came into the faith holding a mother's hand, as it were. Mary's mother and an older woman in the church influenced her spiritual choices most. Though she described herself as a "wild lassie," she feared eternal damnation. Hell was very real in her staunch Calvinistic environment; and when an elderly widow warned Mary of her eternal destiny, she vowed she would commit her life to God. Her call to missions came naturally. The Presbyterian Calabar mission in West Africa was well known in her local church, and she grew up hearing the adventure stories of missionaries in Africa—especially her hero David Livingstone—and she vowed that one day she would join them.

Mary Baker Eddy was also introduced to the gospel early in life. The sermons she heard in the Congregational church in New England were probably much like those Mary Slessor heard in the Presbyterian church in Scotland. And Mary Baker Eddy took the message seriously. Indeed, she recounted how God spoke to her personally in her early life:

> For some twelve months, when I was about eight years old, I repeatedly heard a voice calling me distinctly by name, three times, in ascending scale. I thought this was my mother's voice, and sometimes went to her, beseeching her to tell me what she wanted. Her answer was always, "Nothing, child! What do you mean?" Then I would say, "Mother, who *did* call me? I heard somebody call *Mary*, three times!" This continued until I grew discouraged, and my mother was perplexed and anxious.[1]

Her mother finally told Mary to respond to the voice as the boy Samuel had: "Speak, Lord; for Thy servant heareth." What transpired after that is not recorded, but it is entirely possible that God was calling Mary at this time. She responded, but not to follow in the faith of the Bible in which she had been nurtured from infancy. As a teenager she spurned her father's strong views on predestination and eternal punishment. So exasperated was he with her independent turn of mind that he lamented to the local minister that "if Mary Magdalene had seven devils, our Mary has ten."[2] Mary Baker Eddy grew up in the faith, but rejected it for another gospel—outside the bounds of orthodoxy.

LIFESTYLE CHOICES

Other than in their diametrically opposed choices of faith, it is in their lifestyles that we find some of the strongest contrasts between the two Marys.

Mary Slessor went "native." Unlike most missionaries who try to straddle two cultures, she was perfectly content living as an African. She dressed in a sacklike garment, unconcerned about the opinions of outsiders. Nor did it seem to bother her when her adopted daughter Janie removed the chicken from the pot on the fire and laid it on the mud floor while she made the gravy. Mary's ministry to the Africans was all that mattered.

Mary Baker Eddy also lived in poverty during her early adult years, but not by choice. She craved luxurious living, and through the sales of *Science and Health* that's exactly what she got. She owned several homes during her lifetime, but she is most associated with Pleasant View in Concord, New Hampshire, a mansion that drew tourists from all over the country. Even though Boston was her headquarters, she became almost a recluse, remaining isolated not only from the public at large but also from her own followers. She became a wealthy woman who enjoyed every fashion and furnishing money could buy.

CONFIDENT CHOICES

Throughout her missionary life Mary Slessor was a decisive leader and a woman of confident choices. She was a circuit preacher and even a bishop of sorts. But she was more than a religious leader. She served as an arbiter, judging disputes among African tribal leaders as she traveled from one area to another. She was an explorer who ventured into virgin territory to set up trade between the coast and the interior, and worked arduously to improve the economic and physical conditions of the people she served. In 1892 her duties became official when she became the first woman vice-consul in the British Empire.

Mary Baker Eddy, on the other hand, struggled with lack of confidence. While she was the influential founder of a large religious movement, most of her decisions were not characterized by confidence. During her early adult years, when she fell under the influence of P. P. Quimby, a well-known "mental healer" of the day, she would claim with confidence that she had finally been cured of all her ills; then in a matter of days or weeks she would find herself back in her depressed and debilitating state of mind. This roller-coaster mentality continued long after she "discovered" Christian Science. In 1866, while living in Lynn, Massachusetts, she was forced to move eight times during that one year due to problems with associates and difficulty in getting along with friends.

BETTER CHOICES

The weighing of one choice against another in determining what is *better* continually confronted both Marys.

Before she went to Africa, Mary Slessor had served as a lay missionary in the city slums of Dundee, but she could not defend that ministry as God's calling to her. The need was greater in Africa. And later when she was tempted by her fiancé to serve on the coast, already well-served by other missionaries, she wrote: "To leave a field like Okoyong without a worker and go to one of ten or a dozen where the people have an open Bible and plenty of privilege! It is absurd." Mary chose what was better.

Mary Baker Eddy also had opportunities to make *better* choices—geographically and doctrinally—but she failed. Of her, Jesus could not have said, "Mary has chosen what is better." Even had her ministry been orthodox, it was centered in Boston, where there were already plenty of opportunities for folks to hear the gospel. Her converts were not impoverished, unreached people who had never heard of Jesus. They were middle-class Bostonians, most of whom came into her cult from a Christian background. Mary Baker Eddy made choices that seemed good in her own eyes, but they were neither *better* nor *right*.

LIBERATING CHOICES

Mary Slessor was self-confident and never feared being herself. She was outspoken, with a natural sense of humor, and she never put on airs. When walking through the jungle she and her African companions would often sing to ward off the animals. To a friend she wrote, "Our singing would discourage any self-respecting leopard."[3] Was she a liberated woman—a nineteenth-century feminist? She didn't think in terms of feminist issues. She *lived out* her liberation, doing everything and more than any man could or would do. Any leanings she had toward what we think of as women's lib were typically expressed in humor. In the margin of her Bible next to Ephesians 5:22, where Paul admonishes wives to submit to their husbands, she humorously wrote: "Nay, Nay, Paul Laddie, that will not do."

Mary Baker Eddy was anything but a liberated woman. Some would suggest that she subscribed to feminist principles in that she spoke of God as "Mother" and herself as "Mother Mary," the powerful leader of Christian Science. But never in her lifetime was she liberated from the inner struggles that plagued her. She closed herself off from others, always seeking to maintain an image that was not real—an image of a larger-than-life cult personality.

FOOLISH CHOICES

Mary Baker Eddy in many ways was a smart woman who made foolish choices. She was a classic codependent, unable to live without men in her life. She married young, and after her first husband died, she married a man who was unfaithful to her. After her separation and divorce from him, she married again, this time to Asa Eddy, a sewing machine salesman turned Christian Science practitioner. Still her needs were unfulfilled. One after another she brought men into her life, only to see the relationship disintegrate, and she often accused these men of turning against her. In her paranoia she also accused dissident church members of trying to mentally poison her, and in more than one instance she brought such charges into the courtroom. So infamous was her case against Daniel Spofford that it was dubbed the "Salem Witchcraft Trial" of 1878.

Mary Slessor was anything but a codependent woman. Like most single female missionaries, she struggled with loneliness and was tempted to marry. While visiting a coastal town to pick up supplies, she met Charles Morrison, a missionary eighteen years her junior. Despite her eccentricities, he found her attractive. They fell in love and she accepted his marriage proposal, but the wedding never took place. His health prevented his moving to the interior with her, and her commitment to the African people prevented her from joining him on the coast. Marriage to him and to his way of life would have been a foolish choice for her.

MANIPULATIVE CHOICES

It was in the area of manipulation that Mary Baker Eddy excelled. From the time she was a child, she manipulated people to get her own way. Many believed that her "seizures" were less than authentic—a deliberate effort to control those around her. Stories abound of how she manipulated the men in her life. One such story has a touch of humor. When Asa Eddy was asked why his engagement to her had been kept secret until the night before the wedding, he responded, "I didn't know a thing about it myself until last night."[4] She also manipulated her associates, often for financial gain, as was true with the continual string of new editions of *Science and Health*, which every member was required to purchase.

Mary Slessor was too straightforward and honest to be characterized as manipulative. It is true that some objected to her dictatorial style as a judge and that she used unconventional methods in convicting the guilty—such as drawing from her own knowledge rather than relying only on the evidence presented to her—but she was fair, and she never exploited situations for personal gain.

PAINFUL CHOICES

Mary Slessor was faced with many painful choices in life, none less wrenching than the time she had to return from a furlough in Scotland during which one of her sisters had died. Her mother was also seriously ill and another sister was sickly, and these family obligations weighed heavily on her. But her furlough had already been extended far beyond the usual one year, and her family back in Africa—her adopted children and converts—also needed her. The pain of leaving her loved ones was only exceeded by the news that her mother had died, followed soon after by her other sister. Though overwhelmed by grief, Mary accepted it as God's providence and clung even more tightly to Africa, her adopted home. "There is no one to write and tell all my stories and troubles and nonsense to," she lamented. But she also saw the bright side: "Heaven is now nearer to me than Britain, and no one will be anxious about me if I go up-country."[5]

Mary Baker Eddy also made painful choices. As a young mother she gave up her son George to a foster family when, due to her physical and mental state, she could no longer care for him. Surely that must have pained her, but not enough to induce her to take him back when she was able. She was consumed with her own problems, and life was easier without the responsibility of a child. Mary Baker Eddy gave up her son so she could fulfill her own dreams and aspirations.

COMPROMISING CHOICES

Mary Slessor was criticized by some who believed she should have taken more precautions to preserve her own health. Her poor living conditions resulted in occasional fevers and outbreaks of boils. She lived "not only like an African, but like a poor African," according to a biographer, and as such she was susceptible to their diseases. She "went native" by choice, and it was unquestionably a compromising choice. Had she been able to maintain a higher lifestyle than the Africans and still fully identify with them, perhaps she would have done so. But she was committed to being one of them, and that required compromising choices. Yet the motivation behind her choice was focused outward. Her concern was for the good of others—for the community of God rather than herself as an individual.

Mary Baker Eddy made many compromising choices in the area of faith and doctrine—ones that compromised the authority of Scripture. They were compromises in the wrong direction, nourished by wrong motives.

CONFRONTATIONAL CHOICES

Mary Slessor stood up to African chiefs, knowing full well the dangers she faced. "I am going to a new tribe up-country," she wrote, "a fierce, cruel people, and everyone tells me that they will kill me. But I don't fear any hurt— only to combat their savage customs will require courage and firmness on my part."[6] Some thirty years after she had arrived in Africa, the aging Mary Slessor was still pushing her "poor carcass," as she put it, further on into the jungle to stop the terror of tribal war in a manner that only she could, going where no white man could go without armed militia.[7] As a judge she defended the weak and oppressed against those who wielded power, whether it was a tyrannical husband or a tribal chief. "If not in the strictest fact," write her biographers, "then at least in spirit, Mary Slessor's was the court where no woman lost a case."[8]

Mary Baker Eddy also made confrontational choices. She stood up courageously against her detractors in her own organization and against the Protestant establishment in Boston, which called her "the petti-coat pope." But for all her spirited protest, she was on the wrong side of the confrontation.

COMPASSIONATE CHOICES

Mary Slessor risked her life to save little children, especially abandoned twin babies left to die because they were believed possessed by evil spirits. When she could not find homes for these abandoned babies, she "adopted" them—some nine in all—and regarded them as her own children. Mary Kingsley, a journalist who had little use for missionaries, visited Mary Slessor in 1893 and gave a glowing report of her work: "The amount of good she has done, no man can fully estimate. Okoyong, when she went there alone ... was given, as most of the surrounding districts still are, to killing at funerals, ordeal by poison, and perpetual wars. Many of these evil customs she has stamped out. ... Miss Slessor stands alone."[9]

Mary Baker Eddy was not a woman of compassionate

choices. Like Mary Slessor, she adopted a child—years after she had abandoned her own natural son—but she soon renounced him, as she did so many men in her life. It would be wrong to say that she was totally without compassion, but most of her choices were focused on herself. She "discovered" Christian Science when trying to cure her own ills, and the result of this discovery was poorer, not better, health for her followers. Indeed, a recent study shows that Christian Science devotees have a shorter life expectancy than the population in general.

CONSEQUENCES OF CHOICE

Mary Slessor's death in 1915, at the age of sixty-six, prompted sorrow but not surprise. The only surprise was that she hadn't died years earlier. Africa was the "white man's graveyard"—and the white woman's, too. Few had survived as long as Mary in the malaria-infested interior. Her missionary career lasted nearly forty years, a remarkable example of missionary longevity.

But nobody was thinking of that on the morning her African friends learned that Mary had died the previous night in her own hut. As soon as the news spread, the wailing of the women and the mournful beat of the drums imparted a message no words could convey. When the news reached the other missionaries, her well-meaning cohorts came with a coffin to take Mary's body to the coast for a "proper" burial. The funeral was a big event. Flags flew at half-mast, and soldiers lined the streets for the funeral procession.

Mary Baker Eddy's death in 1910 also brought great sadness, along with bewilderment, to many of her followers. The very founder of Christian Science had died. How could that be? Death, like sickness, was not supposed to be real. Nevertheless, her disciples constructed a special tomb at the Mount Auburn Cemetery where her coffin was interred.

But nothing could stop the rumors. While the tomb was being constructed, her body was heavily guarded, and a telephone was installed in the tomb, apparently to be used by the guards. But rumors abounded that it was hooked up for Mary Baker Eddy should she rise from the dead and feel the urge to give someone a ring.

Revivalist Billy Sunday, known for his ready wit, quickly offered a public wager: "If old Mother Eddy rises from the dead I'll eat polecat for breakfast and wash it down with booze."

The British described Mary Slessor as "a tornado." To the Africans she was simply, *Eka Kpukpro Owo*—"Mother of All the Peoples." She left a legacy that lives on today—a legacy of vibrant Christians going on in the faith.

Mary Baker Eddy also lives on today through her writings and through a religious movement that denies biblical and historical Christianity. Because of her choices, countless men and women in America and abroad have been led astray.

Two women. Both had incredible opportunities to reach out with the love of Christ and change the world. One made right choices. The other did not.

> *Dear God,*
> *Be the Wisdom of my choices;*
> *Help discern conflicting voices,*
>   *through the blare of jumbled noises.*
> *In your will, my soul rejoices. Amen.*

Notes

INTRODUCTION

1. Jean-Paul Sartre, "Existentialism Is a Humanism," *Christian Perspectives on Learning* (Grand Rapids: Calvin College, 1989), 94.
2. Sartre, "Existentialism," 107.
3. Richard Lacayo, "On the Front Lines," *Time* (September 11, 1989): 17.

CHAPTER ONE: IMPOSSIBLE CHOICES

1. M. Scott Peck, *People of the Lie: The Hope for Healing Human Evil* (New York: Simon and Schuster, 1983), 121–24.

CHAPTER TWO: ENDURING CHOICES

1. Simone de Beauvoir, *The Second Sex* (New York: Bantam Books, 1961), 90.
2. Charles Ryrie, *The Place of Women in the Church* (Chicago: Moody, 1968), 23.
3. Sartre, "Existentialism," 99.

CHAPTER THREE: SPIRITUAL CHOICES

1. Anne Morrow Lindbergh, *The Gift from the Sea* (New York: Vintage Books, 1978), 42, 48.
2. Elizabeth Sand Turner, *What Unity Teaches* (Lee's Summit, Mo.: Unity School of Christianity, 1954), 8. Italics mine.
3. Priscilla Brandt, *Two Way Prayer* (Waco, Tx.: Word, 1979).
4. Kari Torjesen Malcolm, *Women At the Crossroads* (Downers Grove, Ill.: InterVarsity, 1982), 21–23.

CHAPTER FOUR: LIFESTYLE CHOICES

1. Karen Mains, *Open Heart, Open Home* (Elgin, Ill.: David C. Cook, 1976), 24–26.
2. John Trott, "Homosexuality—No Way Out?" *Cornerstone* 94, no. 9.
3. Harold Ivan Smith, *Movers and Shapers* (Old Tappan, N.J.: Revell, 1988), 166–87.
4. Ibid.

5. Ibid.
6. Ibid.
7. "Phil Donahue Show," August 2, 1991.

CHAPTER FIVE: CONFIDENT CHOICES

1. F. F. Bruce, ed., *International Bible Commentary* (Grand Rapids: Zondervan, 1986), 318.
2. Ruth A. Tucker, *First Ladies of the Parish* (Grand Rapids: Zondervan, 1988), 53–57.
3. Catherine Marshall, *To Live Again* (New York: Avon, 1957), 25.
4. Ruth Peale, *The Adventure of Being a Wife* (Englewood Cliffs, N.J.: Prentice-Hall, 1972), 63–65.
5. David G. Meyers and Malcolm A. Jeeves, *Psychology Through the Eyes of Faith* (San Francisco: Harper & Row, 1987), 130.
6. Tim Stafford, "Roberta Hestenes: Taking Charge," *Christianity Today* (March 3, 1989): 17–22.

CHAPTER SIX: BETTER CHOICES

1. C. S. Lewis in a letter to Arthur Greeves.
2. Dorie Van Stone with Erwin W. Lutzer, *Dorie: The Girl Nobody Loved* (Chicago: Moody, 1979), 132–40.

CHAPTER SEVEN: LIBERATING CHOICES

1. Abraham Kuyper, *Women of the New Testament*, trans. Henry Zylstra (Grand Rapids: Zondervan, 1933), 32.
2. Dorothy L. Sayers, *Are Women Human?* (Grand Rapids: Eerdmans, 1971), 47.
3. Delores Sunda, "We Have Souls, Too," *Alliance Life* (November 23, 1988): 16–17.
4. Twila Knaack, *Ethel Waters: I Touched a Sparrow* (Waco, Tx.: Word, 1978).

CHAPTER EIGHT: FOOLISH CHOICES

1. Allison Hughes, *Love, Honor and Frustration* (Grand Rapids: Zondervan, 1977), 153–54.
2. Connell Cowan and Melvyn Kinder, *Smart Women, Foolish Choices* (New York: Clarkson N. Potter, 1985), 187–88.
3. Nancy M. Tischler, *A Voice of Her Own: Women, Literature, and Transformation* (Grand Rapids: Zondervan, 1987), 29.

CHAPTER NINE: MANIPULATIVE CHOICES

1. Herbert Lockyer, *All the Women of the Bible* (Grand Rapids: Zondervan, 1985), 136.
2. Nancy Gibbs, "Murders They Wrote," *Time* (April 1, 1991): 29.

3. Scott Fagerstrom, "Critics Question Nora Lam's Life Story," *Christianity Today* (January 14, 1991): 44.
4. Loma Dueck, "Dream Turned Fact Launches Best Selling Author," *Christian Week* (June 11, 1991): 8.
5. Gretchen and Bob Passantino and Jon Trott, "Satan's Sideshow," *Cornerstone* 18, no. 90, pp. 23–38. As this book was going to press, Pelican Publishers announced it was reissuing *Satan's Underground* following a "personal review" by Milburn Calhoun, Pelican's publisher, and an investigation that supposedly cleared Lauren Stratford. Mr. Calhoun did not return phone calls seeking information about this review and investigation.
6. Isobel Kuhn, "Vistas" in Carolyn L. Canfield, *One Vision Only* (Chicago: Moody, 1959), 138–39.
7. Anne Wilson Schaef, *Women's Reality: An Emerging Female System in a White Male Society* (San Francisco: Harper & Row, 1981), 45.
8. Marabel Morgan, *The Total Woman* (Old Tappan, N.J.: Fleming H. Revell, 1973), 95.
9. Helen B. Andelin, *Fascinating Womanhood* (Santa Barbara, Calif.: Pacific Press, 1974), 180, 182, 199.

CHAPTER TEN: PAINFUL CHOICES

1. M. Scott Peck, *The Road Less Traveled: A New Psychology of Love, Traditional Values, and Spiritual Growth* (New York: Simon & Schuster, 1978), 16.
2. Dorothy Clarke Wilson, *Climb Every Mountain: The Story of Granny Brand* (London: Hodder and Stoughton, 1976), 32–33, 42.
3. Paul Brand and Philip Yancey, *In His Image* (Grand Rapids: Zondervan, 1984), 43–46.

CHAPTER ELEVEN: COMPROMISING CHOICES

1. Mark Twain, "The McWilliamses and the Burglar Alarm," *Harpers* (Christmas 1882).
2. Billy Graham, *Facing Death and the Life After* (Waco, Tx.: Word, 1987), 113–14.
3. Patricia Gundry, *Neither Slave Nor Free: Helping Women Answer the Call the Church Leadership* (San Francisco: Harper & Row, 1987), 103.

CHAPTER TWELVE: CONFRONTATIONAL CHOICES

1. Lockyer, *All the Women of the Bible*, 165.
2. Roland H. Bainton, *Women of the Reformation in Germany and Italy* (Minneapolis: Augsburg, 1971), 73.

3. Ibid., 248–49.
4. Ibid., 105.
5. John Winthrop, "Short Story," in David D. Hall, ed., *The Antinomian Controversy* (Middletown, Conn.: Wesleyan University Press, 1968), 213.
6. Elisabeth Elliot, "The Essence of Femininity: A Personal Perspective," in John Piper and Wayne Grudem, *Recovering Biblical Manhood and Womanhood* (Wheaton, Ill.: Crossway, 1991), 397.
7. Jack Houston, "The Jerald Tanners vs. Mormonism," *Power for Living* (June 14, 1970): 3.
8. Ibid., 6.
9. John Gutman, "A Mission of A Different Kind," *Salt Lake Tribune,* (January 27, 1985): 4S.
10. Ibid., 6S.

CHAPTER THIRTEEN: COMPASSIONATE CHOICES

1. Rodney Clapp, "Is the 'Traditional' Family Biblical?" *Christianity Today* (September 16, 1988): 26.
2. Sarah L. Anderson, "Dr. Rose: Bringing New Life to Dead Churches," *Good News* (March/April 1989): 16–21.
3. Catherine Bramwell-Booth, *Catherine Booth* (London: Hodder and Stoughton, 1970), 341.
4. Henri Nouwen, "Adam's Peace," *World Vision* (August/September 1988): 4–7.

CHAPTER FOURTEEN: CONSEQUENCES OF CHOICE

1. Edwin F. Dakin, *Mrs. Eddy: The Biography of a Virginal Mind* (New York: Charles Scribner's Sons, 1930), 7–8.
2. Sibyl Wilbur, *The Life of Mary Baker Eddy* (New York: Concord, 1907), 30.
3. James Buchan, *The Expendable Mary Slessor* (New York: Seabury, 1981), 5.
4. Julius Silberger, Jr., *Mary Baker Eddy: An Interpretive Biography* (Boston: Little, Brown, and Co., 1980), 129.
5. W. P. Livingstone, *Mary Slessor of Calabar: Pioneer Missionary* (London: Hodder & Stoughton, 1915), 51.
6. Ibid., 57.
7. Buchan, *The Expendable Mary Slessor*, xii.
8. Carol Christian and Gladys Plummer, *God and One Red Head* (Grand Rapids: Zondervan, 1970), 151.
9. Livingstone, *Mary Slessor of Calabar*, 143.